THERE
ARE NO
WHITE
PEOPLE

ABOUT THE AUTHOR

Onyeka Nwelue is a Nigerian filmmaker, publisher, talk-show host, bookseller, author of 15 books and an academic visitor and founder of the James Currey Society, at the African Studies Centre, University of Oxford.

He is the Dean of School of Cinematographic Studies at Université Queensland in Haiti.

He lives between Oxford and Johannesburg.

THERE ARE NO WHITE PEOPLE

Letters from an African in
Africa to Africans in Diaspora

ONYEKA NWELUE

Abibiman
Publishing

New York & London

First published in Great Britain in 2022
by Abibiman Publishing
www.abibimanpublishing.com

Copyright © 2022 by Onyeka Nwelue

Published in the United Kingdom by
Abibiman Publishing, an imprint of Abibiman Music & Publishing,
London.
Abibiman Publishing is registered under
Hudics LLC in the United States and in the United Kingdom.

ISBN: 978-1-7396934-0-4

This is a work of non-fiction.

Cover design by Gabriel Ogungbade
Illustrations by Frank Anwuacha

for

Professor Henry Louis Gates Jr

CONTENTS

INTRODUCTION

This book was an idea that had been with me for a long time, since I was a child, but which crystallized as these things often do, in the course of my travels. When I first came to the United States of America, I did not allow racism to overshadow my thoughts; with time, however, I came to understand the dynamics of colorism. The door to this understanding opened more broadly when I visited the Republic of South Africa. I felt then that there was a need to address this institutionalized madness.

My parents are both Igbo and Nigerians, but my mother is from Oguta, whose dialect is different from that of Ehime Mbano, where my father comes from. Yet, there is schism between the two cultures: Oguta people call Ehime Mbano people 'drinkers of dead people's water.' Oguta people say Ehime Mbano people eat achi soup and that it is a crime. This is because they don't eat it. Ehime Mbano people despise catfish and Oguta people revel in it. These differences are cultural, but in these areas, they mean a lot to minds that promote segregation and intolerance. Nonetheless, it seems the concomitant spite that our endogenous differences engender diminishes in repugnance when compared to the scourge of colorism.

Colorism is differentiating things. When the Europeans came, they came with these ideas to institutionalize things and 'mark' them. They chose between Black and White – because we always say things are 'in black and white.' We all know what these two colors stand for. They say that when you mix white and black, you produce brown? You produce the colored? I think we produce the confused. Or the confusing. So, the Europeans quickly said to themselves, 'Let's call these folks black, because they are impure.' Hence, why we are called blacks today by everyone.

Who wrote the Bible? Who wrote the Quran? Who made the rules?

Revolutions will happen in this book, because I want to turn the tables. Let's say these guys who call themselves White are Pink; because if you would sit down and look at their skin, they are not White. They have this confusing skin color, that I would simply call Pink. So, from now, until the end of this book, I will address them as Pink, to institutionalize and alternate what they have given to us.

For those who won't understand where my anger comes from, check these words in the dictionary:

1. Blacklist
2. Blackmail
3. Black Magic
4. Black Market
5. Blackout
6. Blackface
7. Black up
8. Blackguard

There are more words starting with 'black' that are negative and clearly stand for illegality or criminality. Pink people created these words – nothing more than hate will make another see people of a different race as illegal. Pink people clearly believe that we are the blood of the Satan, which is designed to be Black. God, in his Infinite Beauty, is apparently White. They chose White for the color of their Skin? For what, exactly? For Purity. They believe they are pure and that Africans are the Blacks, the Illegals. Unfortunately, Africans absorbed this without asking questions. They have never been a people that ask questions. Right when did the colorisation of people start? It started with slavery and colonialism, which are ideas of Pink people. I have had to fight the thoughts of being addressed as

Black. If calling a Pink person Pink irritates them, then, they should know that I am miffed at being called Black, because it is completely derogatory.

Pink people would say, What then do you want to be called?

I will like to be called a human and not black. They do call Japanese people, Japanese. Not by colour.

Black is derogatory. I am not a dog. I don't want to be colorised and named by another person, who calls himself White, because he feels he is superior and pure.

Let's look at these:

1. White wash
2. Whitened
3. Whitelist

These are just three and see how glorified they are. What matters more is the way these words are used to subdue the African. We are always looking for validation from Pink people, who have successfully created the system and enslaved us. This is not to say that we don't know what we are doing and that we can't free ourselves mentally.

ON MEETING JANE ELLIOT

If you have heard of Jane Elliot, the lady who did the Blue Eyes-Brown Eyes Experiment, that was first conducted on the morning Martin Luther King was killed, you would not drop this book, because you feel it is racist – you will, understand, that I am trying to dialogue with Pink people, so they can stop beaming with superiority.

On the day I visited Jane Elliot in her Sun City estate in California, I knew I was going to learn a lot. She welcomed me into her home and we had lunch and then dinner. She even asked me to stay another day, so our conversation could continue. I did. The two days I spent in her house, inspired this book. Even though I would say that I had been wombing the idea of a book that would address the issue of colorisation and slavery and colonialism, comparing and contrasting today's views on gender and sexuality.

"Every white child is born racist," Jane Elliot said to me in her sitting room. I looked at her. She was wearing a white shirt – her skin was far from white. Her skin, was a mixture of colors. I could see pink, green, blue. When you add up these colors, she is definitely pale. Here is the thing: this is not to make mockery of any race, but there is nothing White about

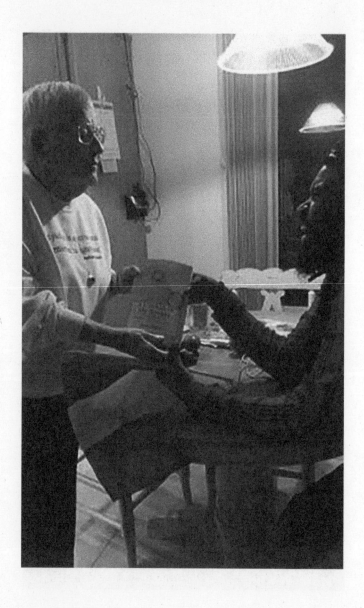

White people. They have no defined color. And that could have formed the idea of imposing some color on Africans.

What exactly is Black and White? Who came up with these colors if not some rabid religious person, trying to pan a race for the color of Satan and another for God.

Satan is Black.

God is White.

Jane Elliot did not realise how much it hurt me when she said those things and validated the colorisation of a people. She may have been speaking for the 'oppressed' but if the educated class of the Pink race, keeps repeating the mistakes of their ancestors, I have no other choice but to also rewrite the narrative. For how long are we going to allow Pink people define us? Choose standards for us? We are clearly a creation of Pink people. It could be flattering to have had a long live-streamed chat with Jane Elliot, but I came out, feeling inebriated by the idea that we have to remain what we have been called.

For Jane Elliot, I was the first 'African' she was meeting. She had been with African-Americans. Larger percentage of African-Americans will be shocked to know that their ancestors came from the Western region of Africa, because of their physique and stature. Many of them won't realise this, but the only difference between a West African and an African-American is the lightness in skin color; yet, many of these African-Americans could be said to have come from the Igbo tribe of Nigeria, where the people are usually with lighter skin. How this happened? I will explain.

The West Africans are naturally greedy and gullible people. They spend time, fighting themselves. There is an unhealthy obsession about Nigerians exhibited by Ghanaians. Yet, these two countries do not share a border. Many people have tried to correlate this unfortunate behavior to the way Ghanaians treated Nigerians and how Nigerians treated Ghanaians in the past, by massively deporting themselves. Oh well, it does not really work out that way in my understanding of the feud. It is just a natural thing that West Africans, unlike the East Africans and the Southern Africans, could, boldly and gloriously, betray their brothers and sisters, snitch on them and sell them into slavery, for whatever it is worth. We will delve into this in the next chapters of the book, but now, let me stick to explaining why this is a West African thing; these traits of betrayal and angst you can find in the African-American, that tendency to be aggressive and hateful.

We have blamed the Pink people enough for slavery and colonialism. This book is my way of saying: Let us take responsibility for our failures and shortcomings.

When I was 7 years old, my grandmother once said to me: "If this was during slavery, we would have sold you into slavery, because you are lazy."

She died two years later.

I grew up in my village, on a farm. I spent a lot of time with my grandmother. I loved her. She loved me. She would always keep leftovers of her food for me.

And she was right. I would have been sold into slavery because I could not farm. I hate carrying shovels or hoes to farm with them. I would feign illness whenever it was Friday, because we were sure to be driven to the farms on Saturday, in different directions. Me and my siblings. And those who did well on the farms were praised. My father had gotten angry once and suggested that I would not be able to raise a family, because I was lazy. He said that my younger brothers were stronger than me.

If it was during slavery, I would have been sold.

When West Africans were selling their 'lazy' sons and daughters, they may not have collected money. They were trying to discipline them. They would hand over the 'lazy' ones to Pink people, who would sail away to the Americas. These families said that if these 'lazy' ones worked in the Pink people's plantations, they will become hardworking and strong. They wanted to punish them by sending them away for a while to work and get strong. These ones that were sent away, never returned.

They are the African-Americans.

It is debatable, but for those who have lived in West Africa, these striking resemblance and similarities between the West African and the African-American are to be cherished and looked deeply into.

I've gotten into arguments with African-Americans in the course of which they suggested I am a 'Low-Life Nigger.'

The only word I could muster was 'Slave.'

Slavery was done out of our volition. Africans had the choice to revolt and resist the Pink people. This is where I agree with Kanye West, when he suggested that 'Slavery was a choice.' It is still a choice. Let me address some things right now.

West Africans sail through the Mediterranean to Europe. Many die in the seas. They are encouraged by their families to embark on this unpleasant journey. They are eager to go through what their brothers who were taken into captivity and slavery went through, on their own. It is okay to argue with me on this, but why do they have to voluntarily subject themselves to such medieval punishment? Let me articulate this properly. Maybe, I am not.

Nigerian women, when they are pregnant, will do anything to have their children delivered in the United States, so they could become American citizens.

What part of self-enslavement have we decided to ignore in this narrative?

Let us look at how gullible we have all become when people pay millions to get a visa to travel to the United States from Nigeria, travel and abscond to seek asylum? There is a huge number of people doing this from West Africa. It was disheartening to see people attack Kanye West for his views, knowing truly that he was saying what was meant to be said but not meant to be heard. We always say they came and plundered our lands. This is absolute bunkum. Pink people are not that smart – at least from the findings of Jane Elliot, people with brown eyes are smarter than people with blue eyes. I agree with her, but in the case of the narrative on slavery, it makes us look stupid.

In 2011, I had invited two people from The Netherlands to Nigeria, to work on a film project with me. When they arrived, the weather was not nice for them. They kept turning to different colors. Their skin color would become pale this morning and by afternoon, it was pink and that in the evening, it will turn green. I was worried about them. Then, they ate oji – which the Igbo people call kola nut in English. Oji is medicinal and bitter. When you eat it, you will frown, but there are also people who eat it deliciously and amiably. So, these Dutch filmmakers were offered palmwine and kola nut; they ate them and drank palmwine. We ended up taking them to the hospital. They were obviously allergic to these things.

Years later, when I had arrived the United States, I would say to myself: how come our ancestors could not kill all Pink people with kola nut or even offer them more toxic stuff to eat?

No, they would not. They were okay welcoming strangers into their homes and showing them that they were hospitable people. To what end? They left with their brothers and sisters. Shipped away. Sailed away.

Africans ought to apologize to African-Americans for this negligence and madness of our ancestors.

This book is a series of letters, apologizing to African-Americans for what we did. We must begin to take responsibility for what we did.

THE ENCOUNTER

Which brings me to Professor Henry Louis Gates, Jr, whom I had met in Harvard when I travelled to attend an event in honour of Nobel Laureate, Wole Soyinka, who was Gates' PhD director at Cambridge.

For years, I had followed the writings and documentary work of 'Skip' Gates, Jr and wanted to meet him badly. Years ago, he faced a ferocious backlash when he suggested that Africans sold their own people into slavery. He was attacked front, back and center for that view. He was attacked by people who knew he was saying the truth. African intellectuals tend to hush anyone that suggests that, but what would have stopped a people from protecting their own? They claim that Pink people came with guns, but we had Dane guns, several ingenious metal weapons, and even what would have passed for weapons of mass destruction. Sometimes, we made it look like there were no internal battles in West Africa then. That all we did was have sex and make children and eat and farm. This is not true. We had battles, too. We had weapons. We fought ourselves. How we were not able to fight Pink people, amazes me.

Strangely, Pink people want to stick to the narrative that they defeated us, so they can have more power. That is not true. We Africans had options that would have enabled us

Henry Louis Gates Jr ✔ @He... · 5/10/18 ∨
Monday, I had the great pleasure of
meeting with award-winning writer,
filmmaker, and educator @onyekanwelue
at the @HutchinsCenter @Harvard. He is
currently developing a documentary film
on the life of Wole Soyinka, which I am
very excited for! Thanks for coming by,
Onyeka!

You

♡ 1   ⇄ 17   ♡ 105   ⬆

destroy the invaders. In light of that, one question we need
to ask is this: were they really invaders? We gave them rooms
to sleep in, food to eat, water to drink, women to sleep with
and even married off some of those beauties, and then, when
they were leaving, we handed our 'lazy' brothers and sisters
to them.

Only if we can accept that we are heavily implicated in the
enslavement of our people, then we will begin to take reproach
and accept responsibility for where we failed. If this is not
done, West African nations, with slave ports, will remain in
total shackles and shambles and absolute underdevelopment.

THE LETTERS

My dearest Sibling in Diaspora,
I'm writing you these letters from Africa, a place described as a jungle by Pink people.

It was from there that your great-grandfathers and mothers were chained and shipped away – against their will – to lands culturally different from theirs. They were forced into outfits that were strange to them. They were made to live in a different climate, against their will. They were mullioned, decorated and had a new life festered on them. A very different life. More chaotic than they ever lived; translucently debilitating and quite horrendous; more often than you would find in the hardship that young people who are trafficked through Libya to Europe via the Mediterranean experience today.

When I look at the videos and pictures, I cringe. Some of these people chose that route, because they would have been refused visa at the embassies of these European nations. They decide to make the journey via the sea and when they get into trouble, the 'European Saviours' will come to 'rescue' them.

When Europeans stop playing God, I shall know.

I am writing to you with a sorrowful and angry soul, because what the Pink people did to our fathers and mothers

must never be forgotten or forgiven. We shall keep demanding that they apologize, and ceaselessly remind them of their crimes against humanity. These are tasks we must discharge daily. If we fail to do those, the Pink people would continue to manipulate and wound us. The Pink persons are evil; they constitute an affliction upon the world. Their heartlessness is unrivaled. Therefore, we must zealously repulse their advance.

I am only writing to you, to apologize for many misdeeds. I apologize to you, my dearest African-American sibling, whom we allowed Pink people to take away from us. They have said that we 'sold' you into slavery. I agree. We did, because if we hadn't, no complicity would have been involved in stacking you on the ships. We helped them take you away. This is why I am writing this letter to you…

To say, 'I am sorry' and that you must forgive us for allowing them to take you away.

'Forgive us.'

Right now, there is no 'but' to whatever we did. We have done our best to deny our role in the slave trade. We have tried so hard to shift the blame to Pink people – without taking responsibility for the part of the pie that we ate. We are doing our best to dissociate ourselves from the narrative that pins us to the evil that we helped create.

You might be shocked that I refer to 'white' people as Pink people. Oh well, there are no White people. There is nothing white about their skin colour. It is criminal for anyone to claim to be what they are not. The term, White, was chosen by them for themselves, to identify themselves as the pure race, the innocent ones, the superior ones, the clean ones. And when you confront this banality, they say it is metaphorical. They also tell you to not be overly sensitive, that it is 'politically correct.' Then, you ask them who crafted the political correctness, they go mute. Their reaction to you calling them Pink, which is the true colour of their skin, makes them turn Red. It's confusing.

They termed us 'Black' to brand us as inferior and illegal. Black usually connotes gloom and doom. Few phrases that start with black are positive or uplifting. There is 'Black Friday.' The deadly epidemic that ravaged Europe in the 14th century is termed 'the Black Death.' Apposite is the poignant reflection of the African-American phenomenon, Maya Angelou in her essay, 'Art for the Sake of the Soul' made the observation: 'Some white people actually stand looking out of windows at serious snow falling like cotton rain, covering the tops of cars and streets and fire hydrants and say, "My God, it sure is a black day."

I intend to continue interrogating them, reminding them that their skin colour is not white. Their skin is Pink; hence I continue to address them as Pink. I know they dislike being called Pink, however, they must be called what they are, until they stop calling me Black, or have that absurd description deleted from their misleading dictionaries. However, before I proceed to go into more detailed reasons why I wrote you this letter, I wish to share a certain poem of mine with you. It's called *Do Not Colour Me*, and it's reproduced here.

Don't colour me black
My skin is not black
I am not black
I radiate
When I call you Pink, which is the colour of your skin
You turn red, because it angers you
Don't colour me black
It miffs me, it irks me. Don't.
I warn you. Because aggressive you'd call me.
Don't colour me black.

I find it lampooning. Call me what I want to be called.
I have a name. My race is not black.
If you do not stop it, I shall continue calling you Pink;
That which suits your skin.
If you find it derogatory, I find black so
Don't colour me black
Because you say you are White, which is Pure.
And black is impure and illegal.
Don't colour me black.
Don't colour me black.
Don't.
Colour.
Me.
So, I don't call you Pink,
Which will make you turn Red.
And pale.

Long ago, there was the philologist who, hating the people of Abyssinia, and the Berbers and the Moors, decided that their skin colour was black.

I will tell you a little about the Berbers. The gradation of their skin colour is the darker hue. They occupied Mṛṛakc (which is now spelt as Morocco) and the Nile and the River Niger area, the plains of Timbuktu; its flora and fauna, the Sénégal and Falémé Rivers, down to Ouidah. They were the nomads of the region; explicitly travelling by foot and spending days in the bush, eating roast meat, which they made off the birds and animals they hunted. They had their arrows, bows and metal weapons. They never killed anyone with it. Berbers occupied the area for thousands of years before the beginning of human records in ancient Egypt.

When the Berbers journeyed through Niger, upwards to

the west of the Nile, they travelled with their trinkets down to Mɾɾakc. On these journeys, they paddled their canoes on the Douro River (present-day Vila Nova de Gaia), which flows into the Atlantic Ocean in the north of what is now Portugal. It was on one of these journeys that the Berbers discovered a group of seemingly archaic people, dressed in hideskins and concealing themselves behind trees, and, with their knowledge of Latin, which was developed in Kemet (now Egypt), communicated with them. Importantly, the Berbers were very intelligent and smiled a lot. The Berbers were courteous and respectful to the strangers they had seen and treated them with respect, educating and also learning their culture and understanding their behavioural patterns. It was the Berbers who lifted the light-skinned people they found at the Douro River and interchangeably procreated with them. Some of them returned to Kemet with their children, who are presently the people occupying Egypt.

My problem is with terminology. From my findings and research, done for years, to eliminate the mental inhabitation of the English misery, I jettisoned that it is important to address the narrative of the World by the West, beginning from the ineffable drama of what they have decided to tag World War 1.

My question is: how is the war among the tribes of Europe a World Affair? The reason why the war began didn't concern Igbo people or Yoruba people or Hausa people or the Tivs or the Ijaws or the Binis, but the incurably vapid Pink person thought it was important to call it a World War.

That same year that Lord Lugard decided to bring all the tribes of Nigeria together and lord over them, in 1914, was when some guy was shot in Europe and the war began among them. But they needed their slaves to fight the war. The truth is that there have been Third War, Fourth War and Fifth War since, but this is simply because it does not concern the West anymore.

Let me give you a little background of what they now termed World War 1 and you can tell me if this isn't madness for the kind of terminology they used.

There had been tensions amidst the tribes of Europe—especially in the troubled Balkan region of southeast Europe—for years and this led to what they termed as World War 1. A number of alliances involving European powers, the Ottoman Empire, Russia and other parties had existed for years, but there was a political instability in the Balkans, especially in Bosnia, Serbia and Herzegovina and this threatened to destroy the agreements they have had as tribes. So, in Sarajevo, Bosnia, was where Archduke Franz Ferdinand —heir to the Austro-Hungarian Empire—was shot to death along with his wife Sophie by the Serbian nationalist Gavrilo Princip on June 28, 1914.

Princip and other nationalists were struggling to end Austro-Hungarian rule over Bosnia and Herzegovina.

That was how it all began.

Do you feel sad when you are identified with the colour "black?" You are not alone.

That feeling, rooted in a series of events, pervades the entire races. Let me digress a little. Jane Elliot, a Pink woman remarked for her 'blue eyes-brown eyes' experiment, once told me in her house in California that there was only one race: the human race. I thought about the birds, the dogs, the lions and the trees. There is not just one race. There are many races. That is why we jokingly say, 'You must run your race.' Although these allude to two different situations, they are connected.

There are races in Africa: the Igbo race, the Yoruba race, the Bini race, the Ijaw race, the Zulu race, the Venda race. Indeed, there are numerous races, operating in the same connect. The Igbo person is different from the Yoruba person. There might be similarities, but it is misguided to deny the differences, focusing only on us humans, ignoring the animals, who seem sometimes to understand what the world is about.

I shall expound the background to our feelings. First, however, I would pose some questions. Did you know that the African races and the Pink had contacts that have lasted for centuries? Did you know that what drew the Europeans to Africa in the first place has been a major issue of debate for centuries? Do you know that we prepared the enabling environment for – and helped prolong – the Trans-Atlantic Slave Trade? Have you heard about racism and caste system in Igbo land? Before I continue, I wish to add that the caste system in Igbo land is analogous to the British class system. They have the aristocracy/upper-class, the upper middle-class, the middle-class, the lower middle-class and the working class. The working class is widely misunderstood in Africa as the professional or career class. In England, it means the manual, menial labour group at the bottom of the social hierarchy. Indeed, the derogatory phrase applied to the middle classes by the English upper-class is 'the sort who buys their own silver!' The aristocrats pour their tea from silver teapots that had been in the family chest for centuries. They are just simplified and written in a fashionable and refined language.

Have you heard the terms *Osu, Ume, Ohu*? Now, here are some basic facts that should be assimilated before we forge ahead.

Many have opined that evangelism was the main factor that drew Europeans to Africa. That is the biggest lie ever told, because Pink people were in Africa long before the gongs of evangelism were sounded. However, we have always known the Pink person to have much fundamentalism in their blood. They despise the cultures of others, only patronizing those races when it is convenient.

The Europeans came to our motherland in search of Africans to capture and turn to drudges on the farmlands of the Caribbean and the Americas. However, they did not do this alone. They collaborated with those ancestors of ours who sold their consciences on the same table as Esau (if I am allowed an allegory or analogy from the story they peddled to our people from their Bible). Persons captured were shipped abroad, then auctioned and herded off to crushing toil on slave plantations. The demand for African slaves to develop western nations was overwhelming, and our ancestors zealously supplied the human merchandise. They burned and plundered villages, kidnapping and selling their own kin to the Pink customers.

It was in this era that the international commerce designated the "Triangular Trade" flourished.

Oh, you seem lost at the concept, right? That phrase described three transcontinental voyages: the shipping of Africans to the Americas, the transportation of America's raw produce to European factories, and finally, the conveyance of those factories' manufactures to Africa to trade for slaves. It was indeed an efficiently operated triangle.

I reflect on the Siddis of India, whose ancestors the Portuguese shipped to work on farms. To this day, the Siddis still struggle to be integrated into what they term the 'Indian society.' They are basically Africans, their features same as those of Nigerians.

I know this letter comes to you as a shock, but I would

like you to consider it my version of Willie Lynch's letter, *Making of a Slave*. That document teems with angst, hate and blood. It prompts recall of the phrase with which the British Prime Minister, Winston Churchill, mobilized the British Empire in World War II: 'blood, toil, tears and sweat.' My own letter will be subtler. As I am writing to you intimately, consider it a conversation between siblings. It is for your eyes only. Any Pink person, who stumbles upon it, must view it with equanimity. In like vein did we endure the supposed narrative of our people by Joseph Conrad in *Heart of Darkness*. Pink people have used that book to indoctrinate generations of their race. They end up convinced that Africans live in 'a bend in the river,' as was declared by VS Naipaul. That was a man whose skin was brown, but whose brain was obviously a ghastly Pink hue.

I read a lot, dearest African-American sibling. I travel a lot. This letter is informed by my travels in over 58 countries. I am writing from Shashamane in Ethiopia. It is where the Rastafarians live, on land gifted to them by the irrepressible Emperor Haile Selassie. He was a man whom Pink people of Italy tried in vain to cow – he conquered them. Pink people dislike discussing that diminutive and slight African who vanquished them. They prefer to cram their lessons with tales of Mungo Park's heroism in discovering the River Niger. The River Niger is ancient. It was there before the ingress of Pink people. How could a Pink person who came to West Africa in the 19thcentury 'discover' a channel that preceded his birth by centuries? Isn't that culpable falsehood? Shouldn't the Pink people be charged with perjury and fraud?

Let me continue with my thesis, as my digressions might distract you.

I staunchly believe that the Europeans' primary

motivation was to enslave us, and dominate our economic, social and political cycles. They achieved those goals with the cooperation of some brainless skulls that we call 'ancestors.'

Harsh words, but I have always imagined myself in that era. I would most likely have gotten a reputation for violent rebellion. People must be allowed to live as they wish, but such broadmindedness is abhorrent to Pink people. They are always intent on imposing their outlook on others. It is borne of a misguided feeling of superiority complex, as they believe their way is best. The British imperialist, Cecil Rhodes, had the unexampled cheek to write in 1877: 'I contend that we are the finest race in the world, and that the more of the world we inhabit the better it is for the human race.' I vehemently disagree, and this letter to you is my dissent.

After reading James Baldwin's *The Fire Next Time*, I decided it was important to write this letter to you, to apologize and also share your history with you.

You are not black. Black is illegal. It connotes all that is loathsome and doomful. Reject it totally.

You might ask: 'what then should I be called?'

Oh well, you have a name. You were originally African and you can decide to be called African, but, definitely, you must reject the evil tag, *black*, which blights our lives, a creation of Pink people and their wickedness.

Let me continue.

Over the centuries, the evils of Pink people's activities were acknowledged, and denunciatory voices rose from several quarters. The nefarious trade was defended by European apologists, whose hollow argument was that the enslavement of Africans was a mere continuation of what Africans had inflicted upon themselves. Advocates of the African cause countered this, holding that African culture was being subjected to a grave misconception. They held that the pawn practice, called *iwofa* in the Yoruba language, was different from the slavery imposed on Africans by westerners. They explained that the pawns in pre-colonial Africa were not slaves, as they were not subjected to the coercion, tortures, maiming and murders suffered on the plantations of the Pink man. In the African past, a debtor who was unable to discharge his debt would simply work for the creditor as *iwofa* until the debt was paid.

Now I ask: 'what is your stance on the forgoing argument?' However, I urge that before you take a stand, you should remain neutral while I present more illuminating details, as this letter is comprehensive.

Be patient. Give me time to navigate you through this narrative.

The Pink man's apologists also claimed that our people were taken to civilized nations for better lives. This makes me begin to wonder why they peddle this word 'civilize.' They obviously believed in their heart of hearts that Africans were 'primitive', 'animals' and needed to be programmed and domesticated. This notion hurts, because Africans are traditionally a people who don't look down on anyone. Here we are now, battling with the language of another, because most of us now think and function in a European language and with the mentality that comes with it, spurning ours.

To counter this argument, African apologists have noted that if our enslaved kin had found life in the West more pleasant and comfortable than in Africa, they would not have revolted as they did on many occasions. African slaves sent to America rioted, starting from the coming of the first slaves into North America in 1619. However, they were in chains, mentally and physically. They had been abused, sexually and physically. They had been maimed and raped by the Pink slave

33

raiders. What could they have done in such circumstances? Other rebellions would later erupt, including the Denmark Vessey plot in 1822, and the Nat Turner uprising of 1831.

Dearest African-American sibling, some African apologists cite those two revolts as landmarks in American history, although it was the Nat Turner rebellion that achieved success. Consequent upon those two uprisings, American slave owners naturally became terrified of their human property.

The advocates of the African cause have related the forms of rebellion which occurred. In South Carolina and other parts of America, slaves escaped from their places of incarceration. Those were termed 'runaways.' Although in most cases they could not run very far, they hid in bushes and forests, visiting their fellows on nearby plantations.

The Afro Apologists have of course stressed the difficulties in escaping from slavery. Only very few runaways succeeded. Many were killed in the process, or caught and maimed. A certain torture device was having incensed dogs gnaw at the runaway for a certain period. This, you can find in Fred Mustard Stewart's *Pomp and Circumstance*. It has been noted that Africans' rebellion took various forms: acts of insubordination, sabotage, arson, destruction of masters' property, feigned infirmity, seeming senselessness, laxity at work, poisoning of masters. Alex Haley's *Roots* should not be viewed as fiction. Fiction continues to reflect truth, and it is important that young African-Americans are ceaselessly regaled with narratives about slavery, whilst being prevented from growing up with a slave mentality. Those are among the reasons why I write this letter to you.

The acts of rebellion enumerated, compel the conclusion that, contrary to the claims of European apologists, the slaves were not enjoying better lives than they would have had in Africa. Furthermore, I am yet to mention an aspect of 'Southern hospitality.' Dark-skinned slave women were offered to visiting Pink men for their nighttime pleasure. Slave women were also expected to get pregnant and birth another generation of drudges. These were the ploys of a race that hated dark-skinned Africans and found their skin colour disgusting. They heartily devoured meals cooked by Africans, and thrust into the vaginas of African women. Some of the Pink men humiliated African men by sodomizing them in front of their children. All those outrageous acts were borne of discrimination over ethnicity.

I would be glad to argue with anyone over the atrocities of Pink people. However, I refuse to hear anyone say that Africans should simply 'move on' from slavery. That would be both insult and injury to humanity in general.

Some reactions to the foregoing argument are uncertain or contradictory. In this regard, Muhammad Shareef might be alluded to. In his speech about the War of Oppression, he posits that some Africans waged resistance against their oppressors. However, he also presents the theory that enslaved Africans acquiesced in their own enslavement. We shall take time to swallow this bitter pill, but we must also consider the surrounding circumstances.

My dear, I wish to refer you to Ellen Thorp's *Ladder of Bones*, although I was initially loath to reference any narrative by the West.

When the Portuguese arrived in Benin and Warri in mid-western Nigeria, in the 15th century and established a form of Catholicism there, those communities did not oppose them, unlike the Igbo people who would have revolted. The English then came to Benin in 1553, as *Ladder of Bones* relates 'the year in which Mary Tudor entered upon her brief and sorrowful reign.'

There is more to reveal and I shall make myself clear.

Of course, centuries of exploration, slavery and trade between Africa and Europe preceded the concentrated evangelism of the 19th century. The obnoxious trade continues today, as the Arabs (like those in Libya, Algeria and Morocco), have achieved stupendous wealth from enslaving others. The Arabs are known to relish slavery and servitude. They love it when others clean their shoes and kitchens, while they enjoy their leisure, smoking hukkah.

If you must know, for approximately the first half of the 19th century, Great Britain operated a blockade squadron on the West African coast, arresting and towing slave ships to Freetown, where the vessels' human cargo were freed. It was in this drive that the lad who became Bishop Samuel Ajayi Crowther was liberated at Freetown, and in 1864, became the first African Bishop in modern times. I'd stress 'in modern times' because centuries earlier, the son of the King of Congo had been Bishop of North Africa. This might impel recall of the atrocities of King Leopold of Belgium, who killed 10 million Africans, surpassing Adolf Hitler's genocide on Jews. Although European commentators continue to express horror at Nazi vileness, they don't mention the Belgians' outrage in Congo, for they consider the life of an African worthless.

After centuries of European exploratory and commercial presence in Africa, came the epochal Berlin Conference of 1884 to 1885. There is a fine narrative of that scramble in Adam Hochschild's *King Leopold's Ghost*. There is also another story I must share about the cartographer who created the Map of Africa that was used at that conference.

That assembly of course effected the partitioning of Africa, consequent upon the scramble.

In Berlin, Germany, between 15th November 1884 and

26th February 1885, Otto Von Bismarck and other European statesmen vivisected the African continent. Africans were neither invited to the conference nor consulted. The European powers' effrontery is incredible, considering that even in that era, persons of African descent had qualified as professionals in Europe and proven their intellectual prowess.

The Berlin conferees disregarded African ethnic and sociological groupings, marring the kingdoms and empires of the continent. This is where we see the sophisticated arrogance of the Pink person. His crassness is unparalleled. They devised their territorial boundaries, lumping disparate entities together. The territories they forged birthed today's African nations, often composed of divergent groups with little understanding of one another's cultural structures. Of course, the Europeans also infused Africans with 'Western culture.' That phenomenon is addressed in the chapters that follow.

This Berlin Conference took official effect precisely on February, 26th, 1885. The German, Von Bismarck, read out the final Act of the Conference. The Act included the declaration of territories by European powers by virtue of 'effective occupation and spheres of influence.' Do you know what this means? It simply assigned the spatial areas of our continent to the European powers which exercised cultural, military, economic, and political hegemony over them.

The concept of the "Area of Effective Occupation and Sphere of Influence" as contained in the Act, had, even before the partitioning, roused European nations' avarice. This rapaciousness was exemplified in the actions of chartered companies, merchants, explorers and agents, among whom I'd mention Pierre Savorgnan de Brazza and Henry Morton Stanley. That single Act birthed a political dispensation that has lasted for a century and thirty years. It laid the foundation for our self-abasement and poverty, factors which will bedevil us until the conversion of the Jews.

Appraising the evil enshrined in the Conference, Molefi writes that:

> "New forms of exploitation of Africa had been found, and with the decline in the slave trade, the old European traders had discovered that settlerism and colonization could add greatly to their wealth if they simply exploited the material bounty of the continent. African leaders were not involved in this decision. Europe would simply declare its stakes over Africa. Thus, the Berlin Conference was the first European conference called for the purpose of deciding the fate of an entire continent. This had not happened in the case of Asia or of the Americas."

The partitioning or apportionment at the Berlin Conference of course gave some of the European nations territories that were actually larger their home territories. Regarding this, Molefi writes:

> "King Leopold of Belgium had claimed a personal colony nearly eighty times the size of the country he ruled in Europe. Belgium was about the size of the United States East of the Mississippi River. Furthermore, Leopold had never travelled to Congo, yet he could exercise his personal dominion over the territory through his surrogates. It was the testimony of his

surrogates that had convinced other Europeans
that he should be allowed to continue with
Congo as a personal colony."

Relevant here are the exploits of Cecil Rhodes. Describing
him and his views on Africans and their territories, Omer-
Cooper writes:

"Rhode's ambition was not confined to making
money. However, to him money was a means
and a symbol of success rather than an end in
itself. He was a man who found satisfaction in
building it huge, a born empire builder. His
vision reached out for the whole of Africa,
and indeed to the world itself, embracing the
extension of British imperial authority from the
Cape to Cairo which would be linked by trans-
Africa railway and telegraph"

The above shows how a whole continent was subjugated.
The situation that emerged amounted to leaving an entire
continent in the possession of a single man who knew next to
nothing about it.

Similarly, the Berlin Conference gave the European
merchants, missionaries, explorers and adventurers in
Africa, the backing of their home governments. Agents of
colonization were then assured of metropolitan support. They
were empowered to pillage the African continent, as long as
their home governments shared in the gains.

However, despite metropolitan bracing, a certain need
had to be met. The colonizers needed to devise administrative
structures to implement their programmes for Africa. They

realized that a haphazard or laissez faire approach would blight their objectives.

Consequently, the policies of Indirect Rule, Assimilation, and Association were employed. Irrespective of the names given to those administrative methods, there existed one common denominator. It was to make optimal use of all available resources, to actualize the hidden colonial agenda on our continent. Whatever name a colonial power gave its administrative policy, it was aimed at subjecting the populace to economic, political, and social exploitation.

The colonization that was birthed at the Berlin Conference was – and remains – sheer slavery. As we were considered primitive, European civilization and exploitation were imposed on us. Counting on the support of our traditional rulers, the colonizers succeeded in the division of colonies for Direct and Indirect Rule.

You know, my dear, that under Direct Rule, all the levels of government were controlled by the colonial masters. In Indirect Rule, governors, district commissioners and council advisors were appointed from the colonial countries to administer the colonies through traditional leaders. The aim was to enforce and oversee the exploitation of our resources.

This was observed by Madukwe thus:

> "The coming of the colonial rule to Africa, including Nigeria, in particular from the late 19thcentury has been seen as a major factor in the present sorry state of the economic, social, moral and political values. This was as a result of the policy which they put in place in the design to exploit the natural and human resources of the colonized people. In Nigeria, for instance, the indirect rule system and regionalism were

in operation. This colonial policy thrived in the division of the colonized people, especially between the educated elites and the traditional institutions. It also widened the gap between the north and the south in political and educational attainments, thereby sowing the seed of discord in the emergent nations. Thus, it thrived in segregation than in integration of the various socio-cultural groups."

Having gone thus far, the question was how to deal with our religious lives. It was glaring to the Europeans that the religious lives of Africans, if not properly handled, would obstruct thwart the imperialist strategy. Consequently, to achieve their end, they proceeded to fuse religion with politics. Christian missionaries would be protected by European governments, so long as their teachings made our ancestors submissive to colonial advance.

Ward wrote that: "The colonial system came into being because a number of people in West Europe, holding certain ideas in matters of religion, social policy, politics and economics, came into contact with African peoples holding different ideas and living under a different system."

When the goal was achieved, we became nothing but strangers in our own lands. The lamentable result of this was that, even many decades after 'independence' (which we still don't have, as it is delusional to say we do), the gap between the West and the countries of our continent is ever increasing.

From all indications, we shall remain slaves to Pink People.

One can see that the coming of Pink People was invasive to our ancestors. However, when they came, many of our avaricious forbears toed the line of 'Esau.' This is coined from their fairytale and myth, focusing on the Bible, which was handed free to every African they could meet (When they arrived in West Africa, the populace could not read the English language. How could they have given them Bibles to read? I know that Archdeacon Dennis was responsible for translating the Bible into Igbo, and another Briton translated it into Efik, ruining his sight in the process). Of course, today Bibles are sold and not handed out freely.

As religious indoctrination spread, few realized that a revolution was underway. When realization dawned, it was too late for the situation to be reversed. We had been plundered and drained. Almost all the challenges faced by our continent are traceable to the presence of the Pinks. To prove this, let us examine the concepts of slavery and caste system, (which we call *Osu*, *Ume*, *Oru* or *Ohu* in Igboland), Colonialism, Capitalism, Politics, Religion, Tribalism, Language, Music, Culture, Migration and Terrorism. Studying those concepts should enrich your mind. You would then understand why I took the trouble to write to you, dearest African-American.

Finally, you would learn how the Pink created and deployed the structures that keep us impoverished till date.

Again, I am moved to apologize, and I hope you find it in your heart to forgive us, while I try to show you how the Pink created and deployed the structures that keep us impoverished till date.

Love,

ONE

ON SLAVERY AND RACISM

I know how you feel. I have met and dined with many of you. I know the stigma you endure in the adopted land of your ancestors. I know your psychological plight. Many of you are seen as monsters, bogeymen, and so on. I know what many of you deserve. Like the proverbial chick under the strong claw of the heartless hawk, I know you need your voices to be heard. There is no way you can come back to Mother Africa and easily trace your ancestors. As I said earlier, I know what you deserve: an apology. Our ancestors must apologize to you. But since they are no more, we your brothers (and sisters?) in Africa really must apologize to you. Personally, I am sorry that we in the land of Africa have not acknowledged this fact. This is why we have misplaced our priorities. We have been selfish. We are advocating that the Pinks should compensate us for the Slave Trade. We have not considered how you, whose ancestors were sold, feel about it, especially those brothers who were directly involved— who are now dead. I think of those who died in the anguished march to the coast; those who died in the hold of ships or were drowned in the Middle Passage; those who perished in the plantations of the West

Indies and Americas. We really need to apologize to you. I say we must apologize to you first, before seeking compensation from the Pink man, because we betrayed you. We captured you. We dehumanized you. We sold you. We prolonged the Slave Trade more than it should have lasted. Despite all that, we are demanding reparation. This is to say that we are still considering you as "wares."

I know I may be sounding strange to some ears, so I want to explain further. I want to reveal some truths to you, taking you back to history to unravel how it happened. I want to tell you a story of how what was 'Local Business' in our land was internationalized and how it resulted in your status as Afro-Americans. I want to tell you how your communities were plundered by African brothers just because of European mirrors, umbrellas and other trifles. I want to tell you how we regarded some of you as lesser humans. I want to tell you the evils we did to you. I cannot keep priding around, asking the Pinks to do the needful when I have not admitted my own faults and apologized. I want to tell you how we in Africa participated and prolonged the iniquitous trade that forcefully took you overseas.

Several hundred years ago in our home Africa, our traditional economy teemed with trade, craft and agriculture. Elizabeth Isichei was describing her part of Igboland when she wrote that our people, especially those in my village, Urunnebo, are called "Owaofia wapulu ezi," meaning *People who travelled into distant lands.* This is because our people were long-distance traders who dealt in such commodities as slaves, *ufie* (a red substance people rubbed on their skins), livestock, salt, iron implements and, later, palm produce. Our people traded extensively in slaves. It was a dangerous trade, but very profitable. Yes, we traded in humans then. This, no doubt, provided a fertile ground for the overseas trade in humans. At this juncture, I know you may be wondering how those who were sold as slaves were procured. Regarding this, she shared a story of what her father told her:

"My father told me that [on] one occasion he followed his father on one of these expeditions that took them from Enugwu-Ukwu to Agbaja, and thence to Ubulu, and then to Eke Imoha in Abakaliki. When they came to Agbaja, one man wanted Ozo title to be conferred on him. He said that the members of his age grade were deriding him because he had not taken an Ozo title. This man had to sell two of his children in exchange for the Ozo title. There was another episode when a man had so many children, and he had to ask them to buy one of his children in exchange for one cow. But, whatever the case was, these children were not told that they had been sold. Their parents would ask them to help their family friends convey their goods to market. These children were pampered until they got to Afo Nkwuleto market, in Ubulu where slaves were sold openly. My father continued that when they arrived with these children in this market, they were asked to look after a few worthless commodities. Then the slave dealers, mostly Aro people, would pretend that they were pricing those goods, when they were really surveying the children. They then came back to my father and grandfather, and a price was fixed—some items of European goods. My father said that after they had received these goods they disappeared, and that was the last he saw of these children."

Now, one wonders why a rational African would agree to trade human beings for mere European goods. This puzzled Edaoto Agbeniyi, informing his stance that the incredible, needless incidents that occurred about 400 hundred years ago on our lands could hardly be described as 'trade.' As a people to whom human lives meant much, it should have been very difficult for our people to engage in such barbaric trade as selling humans for liquor, gunpowder and mirrors, prompting all the lies peddled by our conquerors.

Most of those people sold into slavery were either kidnapped or captured in war. One then questions how this kidnapping was made possible. The experience of Olaudah Equiano is illuminating:

> "When the grown people in the neighbourhood had gone far in the fields to labour, the children assembled together in some of the neighbour's premises to play, and commonly some of us used to get up a tree to look out for any assailant or kidnapper that might come upon us, for they sometimes took those opportunities of our parents' absence to attack and carry off as many as they could seize. One day, as I was watching at the top of a tree in our yard, I saw one of those people come into the yard of our next neighbour but one to kidnap, there being many stout young people in it. Immediately on this I gave the alarm of the rogue and he was surrounded by the stoutest of them, who entangled him with cords so that he could not escape till some of the grown up people came and secured him."

Further on this, he wrote that one day, when his people had all gone to the farm, leaving only him and his sister in the house, two men and a woman intruded and abducted them. The captors were too fast and strong enough to muzzle their mouths so that they could not scream to attract people as they were carried into the nearby forest where they were tied up, journeying in that state for the whole day.

In her account, Isichei further wrote that "The destination of slave trade depended on the ages of the slaves. For instance, kidnappers did not carry their victims far because of the fear that they might be caught, or that their victims might overpower them. In such cases, you know that the slave dealers must have tipped the kidnappers and would be waiting in a nearby place. But those who committed crimes or breaches of taboos were carried off by the agbridu people (law enforcement officers) and sold at Ifite Nibo market, near Awka."

In the case of Equiano and his sister, they were children who could not put up effective resistance, which explains why their captors took them very far. It was such that when Equiano saw people from a distance and tried to cry for assistance, he was shoved into a large sack. After days of journeying to an unknown destination, he was finally separated from his sister and, according to him, was sold from one master to another, who were all Africans. This argument was buttressed by Equiano who wrote that "from the time I left my own nation, I always found somebody that understood me till I came to the sea coast. The language of different nations did not totally differ, nor were they so copious as those of the Europeans, particularly the English. They were therefore easily learned, and while I was journeying thus through Africa, I acquired two or three different tongues."

I want to make a point here. I know that some Afro-apologists will come up with the argument that I did not mention that Equiano was treated fairly by some of his captors. Let me state here that there is a difference between trying to stop a child from crying because strangers are around, and giving the child the cuddling he needs as a child. Equiano was only given "fair" treatment by the African slave dealers because they either needed him to be quiet until the next stage of his nightmarish odyssey, or did not want people around to know that he was a slave. For instance, if the happiness of this young slave had mattered to the dealers, why was he cruelly parted from his sister whom he claimed was the source of the little happiness he had? He further writes:

> "I had been traveling for a considerable time when, one evening, to my great surprise, whom should I see brought to the house where I was but my dear sister! As soon as she saw me, she gave a loud shriek and ran into my arms. I was quite overpowered: Neither of us could speak, but for a considerable time clung to each other in mutual embraces, unable to do anything but weep. Our meeting affected all who saw us, and indeed I must acknowledge, in honor of those sable destroyers of human rights, that I never met with any ill-treatment or saw any offered to their slaves except tying them, when necessary, to keep them from running away. When these people knew we were brother and sister, they indulged us to be together, and the man to whom I supposed we belonged laid with us, he in the middle, while she and I held one another by the hands across his breast all night; thus for a while we fought our misfortunes in the joy of being together: but even this small comfort was soon to have an end, for scarcely had the fatal morning appeared when she was again

torn away from me forever! I was now more miserable, if possible than before. The small relief which her presence gave me from pain was gone, and wretchedness of my situation was redoubled by my anxiety after her fate and my apprehensions lest her sufferings should be greater than mine, when I could not be with her to alleviate them. Yes, thou dear partner of my childish sports! Thou sharer of my joys and sorrows! Happy should I have ever esteemed myself to encounter every misery for you, and to procure your freedom by the sacrifice of my own. Though you were earlier forced from my arms, your image has always riveted in my heart, from which neither time nor fortune has been able to remove it...."

From the above, it becomes glaring that the African slave dealers had no genuine intention to make Equiano happy. He proceeded to relate his ordeal at the hands of a rich and loving lady. According to him, from his circumstances, he was moved to assume that he would be adopted by the family. However, to his greatest amazement, at the peak of his relief began another phase of horrendous ordeals. He wrote that "in this resemblance to my former happy state I passed about two months; and began to think I was to be adopted into the family, and was beginning to be reconciled to my situation, and to forget by degrees my misfortunes, then all at once the delusion vanished; for without the least previous knowledge, one morning early, while my dear master and companion was still asleep, I was wakened out of my reverie to fresh sorrow, and hurried away even amongst the uncircumcised. Thus, at the very moment I dreamed of the greatest happiness, I found myself most miserable, and it seemed as if fortune wished to give me this taste of joy only to render the reverse more poignant. The change I now experienced was as painful as it was sudden and unexpected. It was a change indeed from a state of bliss to a scene which is inexpressible by me, as it discovered to me an element I had never before beheld and till then had no idea of, and wherein such instance of hardship and cruelty continually occurred as I can never reflect on but with horror."

All of these true experiences of an African child show the height of inhumane we, the Africans, were that those of us who were not direct victims of the slave trade really owe those who were directly affected. These true experiences of an African child show how beastly we Africans were to our enslaved fellows; a culpability we must expiate. This is the bitter truth the African society never talked about for once. It is the bitter truth that African societies never discuss; instead, we emphasize that the Pink should indemnify us. As Adaobi Tricia noted, we have not considered that our various African families participated in the slave trade; our own reparation to Afro-Americans should be discharged first, before talk of our indemnity. Describing the role and status of her own forbears, Adaobi Tricia wrote that her great-grandfather, Nwaubani Ogogo Oriaku, was a slave trader who gained power and wealth by selling other Africans across the Atlantic. Her father told her proudly that her great-grandfather dealt in palm produce and human beings. According to her, in the late nineteenth century, Nwaubani Ogogo carried a slave-trading license from the Royal Niger Company, an English corporation that ruled part of present Nigeria. At that date, his agents captured slaves across the region and passed them to middlemen, who brought them to the ports of Bonny and Calabar and sold them to Pink merchants. Even when slavery had been abolished in the United States and the United Kingdom his slaves were shipped legally to Cuba and Brazil. His influence and contributions to this obnoxious business drew the attention of colonial officials, who appointed him chief over Umujieze and several other towns. Adaobi further noted that rather than express remorse, some descendants of African slave traders chose to glory in their ancestors' iniquity. She related that she had asked her father (who was a lawyer), if he was not ashamed of their ancestor Nwaubani Ogogo's facilitation of both domestic and international trade in human beings. Her father, irritated, replied: "I can never be ashamed of him. Why should I be? His business was legitimate at the time. He was respected by everyone around...Not everyone could summon the courage to be a slave trader. You had to have some boldness in you."

The foregoing further indicts Africans in the act; it shows that descendants of the African slave middlemen are barely sorry for what was done. That Adaobi was expected to exult in her ancestor's participation in that vile commerce is appalling.

Having read deeply, Adaobi has been moved to ask some questions. She noted that African intellectuals tend to blame the West for the slave trade, disregarding the fact that Pink traders could not have loaded their ships without help from Africans like her great-grandfather. She further wrote that she "read arguments for paying reparations to the descendants of American slaves and wondered whether someone might soon expect my family to contribute." Other members of my generation felt similarly unsettled. She is particular about this because, although the British tried to end the slave trade earlier than it was stopped, Africans were the ones who strove to prolong it, continuing to inflict misery on our continent and those who were shipped abroad.

In Lagos, Yorubaland, there were early moves to abolish the trade, but African resistance ensured its continuance. Adekoya Preye wrote of a period during the 19th century when conditions in Dahomey were causing anxiety for the British Government. In the 1840s, several fruitless efforts were made to persuade the king to enter into an anti-slavery agreement. At the beginning of 1850, Palmerston, the British Foreign Secretary, a passionate opponent of the slave trade, received a deputation from the C.M.S. at the Foreign Office. He also received a letter from the merchant, Thomas Hutton. Both stressed the need to keep Abeokuta's communications with the coast open, and to end the slave trade in Lagos, described as the 'natural port' of Abeokuta. Palmerston passed those views to Beecroft, his new consul, also citing reports that numerous liberated slaves had been kidnapped after reaching Abeokuta, and sold in the Lagos market. The consul was expected to investigate those matters and remonstrate with the Lagos authorities.

One of the Africans who supported the iniquitous business was Kosoko. Adekoya noted that Kosoko, a usurper of the Lagos throne, branded a notorious slave trader, was considered an opponent to legitimate trade and an obstacle to the general advancement of civilization. Adekoya further reported that when Kosoko realized that the British were serious about abolishing the trade, he sailed down the western lagoon to Porto Novo, and later to Whydah. In both places, he became well-known to Portuguese and Brazilian slave traders. He of course pursued the trade, which activity lost him the opportunity to become King of Lagos when accession to that throne was his due. The British supported the enthronement of Akitoye in his stead. Akitoye agreed to end the slave trade in Lagos. Adekoya writes:

> "Beecroft was impressed by what he saw at Abeokuta and by the time he returned to Badagry, he had decided that Britain must intervene in the Lagos dispute on the side of Akintoye. He received the petition he wanted which was duly prepared for Akintoye by Gollmer and it stated thus: '….my humble prayer to you is that you would take Lagos under your protection, that you would plant the English flag there and that you would re-establish me on my rightful throne at Lagos and protect me under my flag; and with your help I promise to enter into a treaty with England to abolish the slave trade at Lagos and to establish and carry on lawful trade, especially with the English merchants… .'Akintoye signed a slave-trade treaty renouncing the slave trade and an identical treaty was signed by the chiefs of Abeokuta on January 5, 1852. At this time, the slave trade in Lagos was noticeably reduced. By 1853, Akintoye died and Dosumu became the next king. However, the people of Lagos recognized Kosoko as their rightful king. It prompted the intensification of the slave trade on the fringes of the Lagos coast. Adekoya further wrote that it was not until Campbell completed a treaty with Kosoko, giving him the port of Palma and a subsidy of 1,000 dollars on the condition that he gave up his slaving activities, that he acquiesced. Campbell also

installed two pro-Kosoko chiefs at Badagry by force, despite the bitter opposition of the Egba who used the port as an outlet for their own trade. As was documented, "Before daylight on Sunday September 28, 1851, Kosoko, with about two thousand followers had left Lagos in about fifty or sixty canoes to Badone, a village on the eastern lagoon about twenty miles from Lagos; and afterwards to Epe permanently."

It was after this that Kosoko agreed to sign the treaty whose 3rd article read thus: "…Kosoko, his caboceers and chiefs do most solemnly pledge themselves to abandon the slave trade, that is the export of slaves from Africa; also not to allow any slave trader to reside at their port, or at any place within their jurisdiction and influence…."

Not minding the treaty signed, Kosoko was said to have naturally taken advantage of the wars still raging in Yorubaland to persist in slave trading. The presence of a British gunboat, however, exerted some control on his activities, as Adekoya observed.

Again, the foregoing has shown that while the slave trade flourished and our kin were shipped abroad, we the Africans were prime facilitators of that situation. Consequently, we should not have the gumption to demand reparation or even apology from descendants of the Pink people who were protagonists of the trade. Adopting Biblical imagery, we the descendants of complicit Africans have not removed the log in our own eyes. As a concerned son of Africa, I wish to take the lead in this situation. I am apologizing to our African brothers and sisters in Diaspora. I also urge fellow Africans to emulate my action. Let us clear our conscience. Let us clean our ancestral messes before asking the Pink to do same.

What else can we say? That racism was also inflicted (and imposed) on us by the Pink? That racism has ended because there is no longer Apartheid? That racism has ended, thanks to the Atlantic Charter? Because there was Martin Luther King Jr.? I wish all those hypotheses were true, but, dear sibling, those are mere illusions. Racism rages on. I do not wish to discuss it on the international level. I wish to talk about it with reference to Igboland in Nigeria. Igboland is in the Southeastern part of the country. Several blacks in the Americas were of Igbo extraction. They were exported because of the racism prevalent in that part of the world. That racism remains alive. It is not termed 'Apartheid' as in South Africa. It is not called by any European name. It is called the *Osu Caste system*.

Let us begin with the seemingly popular notion: Racism was inflicted on us by the Pink. This may be correct, but with some reservations. We, the blacks, have been *racist* to ourselves. It did not start today and will not end soon. What is this thing called *Osu* in Igboland of Nigeria? When did it start? Was it the Pink people's creation? Has it ended? Is it in any way different from racism? If any of those questions should prompt the answer NO, it means we Africans, again, have to apologise both to the Afro-Americans and some of our fellow Africans here on the continent.

Who is an Osu? Overtime in history they were a special group of people that could be likened to present-day monks. In other words, they were people set aside to serve deities. They were considered holy, too. Egbujuo observed that the Osu lived around shrines and voluntarily consecrated themselves to the gods of the shrines. Communities appreciated the deities and, after exploits in battle, donated war captives to the service of the gods. The Osu, traditionally, did not mingle much with others in the society because of their aura of consecration; on the same hand, the 'Diala' (ordinary) members of society, would not risk offending the gods by unrestrained interaction with the gods' devotees. The Osu, therefore married from amongst themselves. Other sources hold the origin of the Osu Caste system as traceable to the early days when the Nri race of Igboland, believed to possess spiritual and mystic powers, went about cleansing people of filth and abominations. It was alleged that any individual, group, or community that refused this cleansing, was regarded as unclean: Osu. Yet another source states that the Osu were people who disobeyed their rulers and were banished. Once banished, they were considered unclean, and prevented from mingling with the rest of society. Some pre-colonial Igbo communities regarded slaves captured in battle as unclean, consequently Osu.

Generally, whatever the origin or cause of Osu institution, one fact was manifest; they could not mingle freely with the rest of society. They were fiercely marginalized, treated as inferior, in some cases as subhuman. This attitude remains in Igboland today.

When slave trade with the outside world started, those that called themselves the Freeborn, otherwise known as the Diala in Igboland, saw it as an avenue to rid their communities of the unclean and ne'er-do-well. Society pounced on them, killing many and selling others into slavery. Egbujuo noted that with the abolition of slavery and the exit of the European slave trader, the Osu populations swelled. They lost every bit of the prestige they initially commanded, becoming an ostracized rather than a consecrated group. Whoever married an Osu became an Osu, the taint following all their descendants. Their stigmatization was horrendous: they were considered vectors of misfortune. The descendants of freed slaves in Igboland were not exempt from this taint, as society continued to call them *ohu*, meaning they retained the status of slaves. Igbo culture forbids their assuming such titles as Eze and Ozo. They could of course not marry the freeborn. To date, families investigate the backgrounds of their children's suitors, forbidding the marriage if a suitor were of Osu or Ohu descent. As far as many Igbo communities are concerned, such persons could never be regarded as full human beings. Adaobi substantiated this prejudice: "My father considers the Ohu in our family a thorn in our side, constantly in opposition to our decisions. In the nineteen-eighties, during a land dispute with another family, two Ohu families testified against us in court. 'They hate us,' my father said. 'No matter how much money they have, they still have a slave mentality.' My friend Ugo, whose family had a similar disagreement with its Ohu members, told me, 'The dissension is coming from all these people with borrowed blood.' " Adaobi further narrated an experience she had as a secondary school child:

> "I first became aware of the Ohu when I attended boarding school in Owerri. I was interested to discover that another new student's family came from Umujieze, though she told me that they hardly ever visited home. It seemed, from our conversations, that we might be related – not an unusual discovery in a large family – but exciting nonetheless. When my parents came to visit, I told them about the girl. My father quietly informed me that we were not blood relatives. She was Ohu, the granddaughter of Nwaokonkwo. I'm not sure if this revelation meant much to me at the time. The girl and I

remained friendly, though we rarely spoke again about our family. But, in 2000, another friend named Ugonna was forbidden from marrying a man she had dated for years, because her family had discovered that he was Osu. Afterwards, an Osu friend named Nonye told me that growing up knowing that her ancestors were slaves was 'sort of like having the bogeyman around.'

Recently, I spoke to Nwannennaya, a thirty-nine-year-old Ohu member of my family. 'The way you people behave is as if we are inferior,' she said. Her parents kept their Ohu ancestry secret from her until she was seventeen. Although our families were neighbors, she and I rarely interacted. 'There was a day you saw me and asked me why I was bleaching my skin,' she said. 'I was very happy because you spoke to me. I went to my mother and told her. You and I are sisters. That is how sisters are supposed to behave.'

All these stories portray the pathetic lot of those innocent people whom society is determined to punish for sins they never committed. Is there any worse racism that that? Of course No. According to Egbujuo: "Discrimination hurts, bruises, crushes. And it must hurt even more deeply when it is inflicted by kith and kin." He further compared the Diala and an average racist when he wrote that "the racist, just like the bigoted Diala, finds pleasure in insisting that Jews or blacks or the 'Osu' are corrupted beings. On any moral scale, neither Botha, Hitler nor Klu Klux Klan conjured the hatred and discrimination being meted to the Osu. This discrimination happens within and amongst people of same ancestry, colour, language and culture. The conceited Diala harbours more contempt for the Osu than the usurping white Australian has for the Aborigines." One is moved to ponder the gravity of this inhumanity to humans in Africa, inhuman discrimination dealt to people of the same nation, language, and other cultural affinities.

Fortunately, people have begun to see the truth. Voices have started asking why this obnoxious practice should not be abolished. People's cruel deeds have started to haunt them. Decent, sound minds are making moves to right the wrongs. An encounter in 2009 between His Royal Highness, Eze E.C. Ekwelibe (Agubiam 1, of Irete Community) and an Osu might be cited. The traditional ruler related: "The encounter was at a village gathering. After drinking palm wine, the eldest man in the village at the time, who was regarded as 'Osu,' wanted to pour out the remnant of that wine on the ground for libation, as the custom requires, but I intervened and stopped him, simply because he was regarded as 'Osu'. He then politely asked me, "Ethel, why are you stopping me"?

And I arrogantly retorted, "Why do you want to do this? Do you not realize that Sunday is here?"

By age and by right, Sunday was much younger and shouldn't be doing the libation. But because the eldest man was regarded as 'Osu', I stopped him and made Sunday pour the libation. Rather than protest it, the elderly 'Osu' man simply said, 'Well, let it be to you people, and you're Christians."

To show how remorseful the traditional ruler became about his mistake, on July 14, 2018, he spearheaded an epochal act in his community. On that day, Ohu, Ume, Diala and 'Osu' Caste Systems were declared abolished in Irete autonomous community, Owerri West Local Government Area of Imo State, Nigeria.

In the foregoing paragraphs, I have depicted some of the effects and scope of the slave trade and caste systems. I have painstakingly portrayed how we, the Africans, dehumanised and selfishly sold our brothers to buy European cheap goods. I have exposed how our ancestors strove and succeeded in prolonging the slave trade, even after the Pink had abandoned it. I declare that, in practising the described discrimination against our own kind, we are racist. What prevents us from admitting our errors? What is preventing us from apologizing to the Afro-Americans for what we did? What prevents us from stopping to discriminate against our own, terming them Osu or Ohu? I state that only when we have done these could we have the moral right to demand apology and reparation from the Pink.

TWO

ON COLONIALISM

Have you ever heard the word 'colonialism?' Do you know its origin? Do you know its meaning? We shall examine how it has immensely contributed in ruining our past, present and even marring our future. Please note, however, that it is a problematic term to define. Ward acknowledged that difficulty:

> *There are difficulties in understanding the history of colonial rule. One difficulty is that the very word 'colonial' – especially the nouns, colonialism' and 'neo colonialism' – rouses strong emotions. Another is the tendency to over-simplify the policy of the colonial powers, such as Britain and France.[1]*

One may, therefore, reasonably conclude that the difficulty in articulating a neat definition of colonialism is caused by the insincerity of the system; the hardship, inhumanity,

---

1   W.E.F.Ward*Colonial Rule in West Africa,*Joseph C. Anene and Godfrey N. Brown eds. *Africa in the Nineteenth and Twentieth Centuries,* (Ibadan: University Press, 1966),308.

exploitation and deceit inherent in the system. We are yet to fully ascertain the scope of decades of European rule, even as the effects remain with us. Thus, explaining the system is difficult. .

Colonialism in its crudest form simply means one country's domination of another country or people – usually achieved through aggressive, often military, actions – and the territory acquired in this manner.[2] It is the direct and overall domination of one country by another on the basis of state power being in the hands of a foreign power.[3] That is to say that the colonized (both educated and uneducated) are all subject to the external power which in return determines the fate of the colonized. The colonized usually have no influence over the politics, legal system and administration of their own nation. One may note here that in most nations during colonialism, the colonizers tolerated 'native' representations in the legislatures. The fact, however, is that most – if not all – the legislative systems established by colonial powers were unevenly distributed, even as the legislatures were merely advisory bodies. The colonizers, who constituted minorities in the populations, occupied huge majorities of the seats in the legislatures. Furthermore, their decisions were always imposed on the colonized. Ward observed that:

> *The great weakness of the legislative councils was that the British did not trust the African members with responsibility. Until 1946, there was an official majority in all four legislative councils, and Africans*

2   Cell, John W. "Colonialism and Colonies."Microsoft® Encarta® 2009 [DVD]. Redmond, WA: Microsoft Corporation, 2008.

3   Basil ChukwuemekaNwankwo, *Colonialism and its Impact in Africa,* African *Politics*: eds. Emezi C.E and Ndoh C.A., Owerri: Achugo Publications 1998).31.

never numbered more than one third of the whole membership; moreover, many of the Africans were nominated, not elected. The position which the colonial government took up was: 'This is what we propose to do, but we shall be glad to listen to your comments if you have any[4]...[5]

The foregoing makes it obvious that Africans in colonial governments were relegated to positions of administrative slavery. They were exposed to the western political system without being allowed to operate that system properly. This was so, because African thought, takes, motions, and worldviews never counted, making it possible for colonial exploitation to flourish unobstructed. Further expounding the goals/stance of the colonizers, facilitated by their administrative system and other structures, Nwankwo highlights two major objectives. First, political domination and second, "to make possible the exploitation[6] of the colonized country."[7] The place of exploitation in colonization cannot be overemphasized, as, from the outset, it was manifest in the methods of the colonial powers. Emezi writes that:

The European Colonial Powers; France, Britain, Belgium, Portugal, Germany and Spain, etc., left no one in doubt that their prime motive for establishing political domination over the hitherto autonomous and sovereign states of Africa, as in Asia and America, was first and foremost economic interest. Since this is hardly controvertible, it would be reasonable to admit

---

4   Emphases are mine.

5   Ward, *Colonial Rule in West Africa*, 322

6   Emphasis is mine

7   Nwankwo, *Colonialism and its Impact in Africa,31*.

that colonial policies and practices in Africa were geared toward optimizing this basic interest.[8]

Emezi further quoted Lugard who writes in his 'Dual Mandate' that:

The partition of Africa was, as we all recognize, due primarily to the economic necessity of increasing the supplies of raw materials and food to meet the needs of the industrialized nations of European....[9]

Emezi therefore summarized:

European colonialism portended negative impact on the African society in a host of spheres: political, economic, socio-cultural and technological. If anything in the form of 'benefits' was ever savored by Africa it was merely incidental to the process of colonial exploitation, for colonialism was ultimately nothing, but complete subjugation of a people![10]

This is to say that colonialism operated to advance the political and economic interests of the colonizers. Observing this, Ward writes that in colonial rule,

There was the colorful career of Sir George Goldie, with his Royal Niger Company: a man with much the same outlook with Cecil Rhodes' in South Africa.

---

8   Cletus E Emezi, *Decolonization Process in Africa: A Critical Reflection,* African *Politics*: eds. Emezi C.E and Ndoh C.A., Owerri: Achugo Publications 1998). 54.
9   Ibid.
10   Ibid.

> *'Open up the country, push the trade, hoist the flag; philanthropy is good, especially if it pays five percent dividends.[11]*

Omer-Cooper has appraised Cecil Rhodes in like vein:

> *Rhodes was prepared to use the slogans of philanthropy when it paid, but normally he thought of Africans, as indeed he tended to do of all men, either as means for attainment of his ends or as obstacles to be removed.[12]*

From that reference to Rhodes, it is obvious that Africans tried in many ways to prevent the colonization of their countries. But all the efforts proved abortive, as in the early twentieth century when most African countries were already colonized except Ethiopia and Liberia. It was very easy for the Pink man to come in and begin his exploits, and of course they were very tactful.

To further explain colonialism, one needs to consider the fact that Britain and France were commercially-driven countries whose traders had, over the centuries, striven to market their wares abroad. Africa's rich natural resources attracted those European adventurers and entrepreneurs. I wish again to state categorically that they were in Africa to exploit us. In order to attain their greedy ends, they urged their governments to establish more colonies which would provide raw materials for trade. Their governments acquiesced, leading to the scramble for Africa by Belgium,

---

11 Ward, *Colonial Rule in West Africa,* 313.
12 J.D. Omer-Cooper, *South Africa from the Great Trek to Unification,* Joseph C. Anene and Godfrey N. Brown eds. *Africa in the Nineteenth and Twentieth Centuries,* (Ibadan: University Press, 1966) 401.

France, the Great Britain, and Portugal, which clamour of course resulted in colonialism. Colonialism, therefore, could be described as "building an overseas territory with the sole aim of extracting resources for metropolitan development, which, in the long run, would impoverish and deprive the colonized of economic, social, and political development." The colonization of Africa is nothing but the attainment of two quests: a ready market for European finished goods, and a source of abundant raw materials for European industries. Those two factors explain why colonization began during the industrial boom in the western world, an era when European powers dispatched explorers and merchants to Africa and Asia. The colonized were indoctrinated to reject their world and embrace that of the colonial power. *West is best* was the credo. Writing on the colonizer's sense of superiority, Ayandele says:

> *Everything about him bore the air of superiority and*
> *separateness. His diet was different, his clothing was*
> *different, his house sometimes may have seemed, to*
> *many African chiefs, more of a threatening fort than a*
> *building intended for a peace-loving stranger.*[13]

Having succeeded in imposing themselves on Africans, the Europeans tactfully tried to present themselves as having the welfare of the colonized at heart. They would give useless products of their factories to Africans in exchange for their lands, elephant tusks, gold, and other precious ornaments. Mirrors, umbrellas and such items were given to African chiefs who did not know how insubstantial those products

---

13 E.A.Ayandele, External Influence on African Society, Joseph C. Anene
    and Godfrey N. Brown eds. *Africa in the Nineteenth and Twentieth Centuries,*
    (Ibadan: University Press, 1966) 135

were. Even over infrastructural developments executed by the colonizers, there was always a ruse. That ploy was to lay a foundation for economic exploitation of colonies. As such, it is no surprise that most of the railways constructed by the colonialists ran from the hinterland to the seaports, to effect the movement of raw materials to the metropole. Instructive is Nwankwo's observation:

> *The transport network developed was not to link different towns and rural areas for purposes of effective communication and development. Transport routes were built by the colonialists to enable them to evacuate easily the raw materials from their sources or base to the destination point where they could be effectively exported abroad. The transport network developed was essentially rails and seaports. There was no good effort to develop an organized road network which would help to improve the lives of the African people and their interaction with their relations in the different parts of the territories.[14]*
>
> In Kenya, *the interest of the British Government appeared to be of building of a railway line from Mombasa to Lake Victoria to speed the exploitation of the economic resources of the area rather than the political and social advancement of the country.[15]*

The selfishness of British interest in this project was observed by Kenyans. They therefore refused to provide the needed labor. Their aversion failed to stall colonial exploitation:

---

14 Nwankwo, *Colonialism and its Impacts in Africa*, 48.
15 *African Year Book and Who's Who 1977*, eds. RaphUwechue*et.al*, (London:Africa Journal Limited Kirkman House, 1076) 495.

Indians were imported to work as labourers. Construction of the railway from Mombasa to Uganda duly began in 1895. By December 1901, the lines' construction reached Kisumu and was finally completed in 1903.

The Gold Coast and Nigeria witnessed similar scenarios. Ward observed that "it took three years to build the first Gold Coast's railway line; the forty miles from Sekondi to Tarkwa, and nearly four years to build the first Nigerian line from Lagos as far as Ibadan"[16] Those projects were not evenly executed for developmental purposes, but rather to serve the economic strategies of colonial rulers.

One of the most inhumane aspects of this bid to develop 'exploitative tracks' by Europeans was that the motives of Africans in setting out their traditional roads were never considered. Prior to colonialism, Africans had constructed their roads to connect their markets. And each road was known for certain goods. Therefore, juxtaposing the lane of infrastructural development in Africa with what the colonizers brought, Nwankwo writes:

> *Colonialism also disarticulated African markets and trades. The traditional or original African marketing centers were distorted by colonialism. Most of the traditional African marketing centers or routes were formed based on local needs. When colonialism came and introduced a different need, this changed the original or traditional marketing centers because it rendered them irrelevant. Colonialists created new marketing centers and routes where their required raw materials could be easily bought and evacuated back home.*[17]

---

16 Ward, *Colonial Rule in West Africa*, 315.
17 Nwankwo, *Colonialism and its Impact in Africa*, 45-6.

Ayandele not only saw the exploitative nature of the transportation networks, but also observed that Africans were not involved in the key economic activities of their own land. They were kept outside the corridors of the economic activities. He writes:

> But one feature of the commercial and industrial activities of Europeans in all Africa is the fact that, until the attainment of independence by many African states, Africans were not participants in capital investment and large concerns such as commercial firms, banking, and shipping. At this point the words of the educated Nigerians sum up the state of affairs: 'you exploit the country with foreign capital and you say you have developed its resources; when capital has deducted its principal and interest, and shipping its profits, precious little is left for the country, and it is that little that is the local wealth...to a poor country like our own where the money comes from abroad, and both the principal and interest will have to go out, I see no advantage, I see impoverishment.[18]

Similarly, Nwankwo adds that:

> Colonialism distorted African pattern of economic development in many different ways. There was disarticulation in production of goods, markets, trades, transport, provision of social amenities and pattern of urbanization etc. the colonialists introduced a pattern of international division of labour which was to the disadvantage of Africans. They assigned to Africans the role of production of raw materials and primary products for use

---

18 Ayandele, *External Influence on African Societies,* Joseph C. Anene and Godfrey N. Brown eds. *Africa in the Nineteenth and Twentieth Centuries,* (Ibadan: University Press, 1966) 145-146.

> *by their industries at home. Africans were not allowed nor*
> *encouraged to go into manufacturing. The only industries*
> *Africans were encouraged to build were those that would*
> *facilitate in the processing of the raw materials for export. The*
> *African raw materials were bought at a very low price while*
> *manufactured goods from abroad were sold at expensive*
> *price. This situation accounted for the impoverishment of*
> *most Africans.[19]*

It cannot be gainsaid that this impoverishment of the African world by the European colonizers was a mustard seed they planted, which has now grown into a mighty tree. The Europeans planned it in such a way that by the time they were done with the Africans, the entire continent was submerged in the abyss of economic wreck. The continent ended up in a situation where it could not surmount any economic challenge without recourse to Western assistance. Successfully brainwashed, Africans remain in that stranglehold. Our export of cash crops depends on foreign countries. Even today, most African countries prefer trade with overseas countries to trade with their neighboring states. This is pure slavery!

With the total exploitation of the continent, its economic development remains an illusion. Africa is flooded with European-made goods, the unfair competition making local industries fail. Europeans exerted their influence to swell the production of cash crops in Africa, causing a drastic decline in our traditional agriculture. Our farmers endured a hellish situation under the dictatorship of Pink People.

Apart from colonialism's economic effects, there also remains the racial prejudice that spread in that era. Planted intentionally by the colonizers, its aim was to inculcate on

---

19 Nwankwo, *Colonialism and its Impacts in Africa,* 45.

the African psyche, the notion of Africans as savages. The Europeans no doubt realized that effective implantation of this colour bar in African minds would facilitate exploitation even after colonialism was officially ended. Describing the role of racism in European colonial policy, Ajayi and Webster conclude:

> On the whole, colonial administration did not favor a liberal policy of education. Beginning from the 1880s, the ideas of racists who believed in the inherent inferiority of Africans, intellectually, morally and spiritually began to be popularized. These ideas fanned up the tide of European nationalism. The partition of Africa was as a search for new economic opportunities but as a fulfillment of the divine mission of the 'superior' races to rule the 'inferior' peoples more or less permanently.[20]

To buttress the point that racism was the anchor of all the colonial policies in Africa, Ndoh in his "Colonial System of Administration in Africa: A Comparative Review" concluded of the Belgian administration in Congo:

> A catastrophe in terms of the evolution of a more advanced system of administration to the indigenous peoples of Africa…her main colonial territory in Africa and this was anchored on racial principles.[21]

---

20 And the effect of this permanence is inherent in nowadays Africa. The psychological colonization of the continent has made the blacks to belief that for one to belong to the global one, westernization is one of the keys. This notions has ramin and is to remain for ages to come. There long run effect is the possibility of the black people to remain 'poor'.

21 Ndoh C.A. *Colonial System of Administration in Africa: A Comparative Review*, African *Politics*: eds. Emezi C.E and Ndoh C.A., Owerri: Achugo Publications 1998), 4.

The Belgian administration of Congo was inhuman from the onset. At an early stage of Leopold's hegemony in Central Africa, he was quoted to have said that "unless by a vigorous authority compelled to work, Africans would quickly relapse into hopeless apathy and indolence…"[22]

Consequent upon that conclusion, the Belgians, with their paternalistic administrative policy, reduced Congo to an administrative state that was worse than a poultry farm. The situation was such that when in 1905 De Brazza visited Congo, he was dismayed and moved to rebuke the Government: "I gave you an empire and you have made a wasteland."[23]

Exemplifying the inhumanity attendant on racial segregation, the Congolese were seen as inferior humans; they were forced to do menial jobs under crushing conditions. A grievous instance was the construction – by forced labour – of the Congo-Ocean railway in the 1920s. It was estimated to have cost 20,000 lives.[24]

Educated Africans were not exempt from the racial debasement. Regarding this, Ajayi *et al.,* observed:

> *Promotion of Africans to the Senior Civil Service practically ceased. The percentage of Africans in the service dropped to its lowest level ever in 1920.* ***Europeanisation became the firm though unproclaimed policy***[25].*African doctors were no longer engaged as government medical officers even though*

---

22 *African Year Book,*, 473.

23 *African Year Book*, 345.

24 Ibid, 345

25 One of the ruses of colonization was that candy-coating was the rule of the game. The Europeans colonizer most often presented to the colonized an inviting plan. The acceptance by the later would then spur the true colour of the colonizers. And at that point, it was too late for the colonized to shake off the shackles.

> *Edinburgh University carried out a long battle with the*
> *colonial office on their behalf.*[26]

Racism was so pervasive that even the church, the hallowed bastion of decency and succor, was affected. Regarding this, Ajayi *et al.,* further noted:

> *The two African bishops in the Anglican Communion,*
> *Crowther of the Niger and Ferguson of Liberia, and*
> *the African superintendents of other missions were*
> *replaced by Europeans. The top ranks of the mission*
> *churches were to remain Pink for the next sixty years.*[27]

This racism, like other attitudes that defined colonialism, continues to impact contemporary Africa. One of the African nations which witnessed virulent racism was South Africa. Having examined racism and its origin in South Africa, Colin concluded:

> *The enduring reality of South Africa's modern historical*
> *development is the establishment and maintenance*
> *in South Africa of an aristocracy in which all Pinks*
> *– irrespective of origin, religion, or accomplishment –*
> *are entitled to share fully, from which all non-Pinks,*
> *irrespective of their accomplishment, or qualification are*
> *virtually excluded.*[28]

Racism in South Africa can be dated back to 1652, when the

---

26 Ajayiet'al, *The Emergence of a New Elite in Africa,* 153.

27 Ibid.

28 Colin Legum, *Nationalism in South Africa*, Joseph C. Anene and Godfrey
   N. Brown eds. *Africa in the Nineteenth and Twentieth Centuries,* (Ibadan:
   University Press, 1966) 420.

Dutch East India Company established a port and decided to settle at Cape. It might be noted that the Company was desirous of maintaining a good relationship with the aboriginals. Consequently, the colony's surgeon was granted a promotion for marrying Eva, a Christian Hottentot woman. One might consequently infer that the Pink settlers were humble folk who were free of racial discrimination. It is obvious, however, that they approved of interracial coupling because they were mostly men, who needed to mate with the available Hottentot women. Similarly, within a short period, in 1685, intermarriage of Pinks and freed slave-women was officially proscribed. Intimacy with Africans was considered disgraceful for Europeans. Additionally, while "official and church policy tried hard to draw a line, not between the races but between 'Christians and barbarians', Van Riebeeck held this to be the proper distinction between 'civilized' and 'uncivilized' peoples."[29] One naturally wonders: who were the Christians if not the Pinks? Who and what defined civilization as used above? Is Europeanization the same thing as civilization? Except these questions are answered, one would not understand the initial ploy of the settlers. In addition to the foregoing argument, the settlers also brought with them the expectation of a material standard of living that was above that of the aboriginal South Africans. The European capitulated on the conception of individual property rights, and the Calvinist religion of mankind into the chosen and the damned.[30]

---

29 Ibid, 421.

30 J.D. Omer-cooper, *South Africa at the Dawn of the Nineteen Century* Joseph C. Anene and Godfrey N. Brown eds. *Africa in the Nineteenth and Twentieth Centuries,* (Ibadan: University Press, 1966) 347.

[31]Of course, despite the rising racism, the relationship between the settlers and the natives appeared cordial for some time. As years passed and European territorial acquisitiveness increased, they began to deprive aborigines of their lands. Aborigines were compelled to work infertile lands, while the European lords and masters enjoyed the choice fields.

This, inevitably, prompted discord between the two groups. The Pinks began to see the native people:

> *More as living instruments than as persons entitled to equal rights. It became unthinkable for a Hottentot to take his master to court and be treated on a basis of legal equality. Religion itself was interpreted to sanctify the status quo, and most simple farmers believed that discrimination between the races was the will of God even if this was not accepted by the official synods of the church.*[32]

As this was going on, the Pink settlers, escalating in number, were increasingly reaching for more. To strip natives of their lands became their passionate goal. The result was that the line of racial discrimination against the Africans grew ever thicker. Before long, "the foundation was laid of a society of masters and servants; of black servants and [Pink] masters; of superiors and inferiors; of people with inherent privileges and others with inherent duties[33]. Examining the emerging events

---

31 J.D. Omer-cooper, *South Africa at the Dawn of the Nineteen Century* Joseph C. Anene and Godfrey N. Brown eds. *Africa in the Nineteenth and Twentieth Centuries,* (Ibadan: University Press, 1966) 347.

32 ibid, 351.

33 Colin Legume, *Nationalism in South Africa,* Joseph C. Anene and Godfrey N. Brown eds. *Africa in the Nineteenth and Twentieth Centuries,* (Ibadan: University Press, 1966) 421.

and attitudes, General Janssens as quoted in *Legums* writes that "they describe themselves as humans and Christians, and the Kaffirs and Hottentots as heathens; and by believing in this they permit themselves everything."[34]

This trend continued and intensified as years passed. By the 1940s, during World War II, the table of division of labour based on colour of the skin was changed. The Africans were then able to do works exclusively reserved for Pink people. When the war was over, Pink people wished to restore the old order which held them to be masters. They felt that to achieve this, new and stringent economic policies must be devised. In the elections of May 26, 1948, the Pink group won enough seats in Parliament. It was this new government, led by Mr. Malan, upheld the Policy of Apartheid[35] to regulate Pink and black coexistence. From then, harsh laws were made against Africans. There were numerous incidents of murder, an instance of which was the Sharpeville Massacre of 21st March, 1960. For no just cause, sixty-nine people were killed and over one hundred and eighty, wounded.

Apart from the political and social assault inflicted on Africans by the apartheid regime, they also suffered economic repression. It was observed of the economic lot of a typical African during Apartheid:

> *The nationalist government also stepped up economic discrimination. Numerous measures were taken to*

---

34 *ibid*, 421.

35 Setting the races apart. It presented separation as an ideology which had to be applied rigidly regardless of any consequences. The word gained political meaning in 1947, when a group of leading nationalists, then teaching at Stellenbosch University, started using it as their election slogan. The National Party then popularized it as the intensification of racial discrimination.

> *consolidate the 'colour bar' in industry, to keep Africans*
> *from holding skilled and even semi-skilled jobs.*
> *The Industrial Conciliation Act, adopted in 1956,*
> *empowered the Labour Minister to 'reserve' any type of*
> *jobs in any industry for members of one race. It provided*
> *the legal mechanism for completely barring Africans,*
> *including all non-Europeans, from skilled jobs. In*
> *1957, the Minister of Labour and Public Works, Mr.*
> *Jan de Klerk, announced his intention of 'preserving'*
> *40,000 jobs for Europeans in the garments industry.[36]*

Although the Apartheid regime ended in South Africa in 1994, the xenophobia that currently rages there is traceable to the rampant racism of the Apartheid past. I state this because the South African psyche was conditioned to believe that forms of discrimination must be practiced wherever different races and nationalities coexist. This retrogressive belief has limited that nation's development. Such divisiveness cannot but hinder national progress.

In this context, it becomes necessary to appraise colonial education. European apologists argue that but for colonialism, Africans would never have acquired the Western education they have today. That may be true any way. That may be true, but Western education and its attendant Anglicization don't amount to true civilization. Africa had educational systems and civilizations before the incursion of the colonial system. The sham of the so-called education brought by the West is glaring. It was an education that despised our traditional norms and practices, urging European values on us. We were submerged in that indoctrination. We accepted that Europeans were the best creatures on the planet, indeed elevated beings,

---

36 *African Year Book*, 792.

and that our innate/inherent inferiority and evil conduct caused colonialism. In all areas, however, the sham of their educational approach was manifest. Apposite are the following remarks about South Africa:

> *The Bantu Education Act, passed in 1953, greatly curtailed the curricula for education in the majority of South African schools. Dr. Verwoerd, then Minister for Native Affairs, remarked cynically that it was no use teaching a Bantu child mathematics since he would never be able to apply it in practice. In 1959, Parliament passed the so-called Extension of University Education Act which prohibited students with different colour skin from studying in the same university. Only Pinks were entitled to study in the existing universities, and special educational establishments were to be set up for non-Europeans.* [37]

The foregoing shows that the education given in the colonial era was a mere shadow of what it should have been. Furthermore, Nwankwo notes that the argument for the positive contribution of colonialism in education "will appear to be true on the surface level or superficially, but if it is subjected to critical analysis, it will reveal the hollowness or emptiness of the colonial education which is partially responsible for the present day African underdevelopment".[38]

He also argued that:

> *The colonial education was not rooted in African culture and therefore could not foster any meaningful*

---

37 *African Year Book*, 793
38 Nwankwo, *Colonialism and its Impact in Africa*, 44.

> *development within the African environment because it had no organic linkage…colonial education was essentially literary; it had no technological base and therefore antithetical to real or industrial development.*[39]

To further buttress his argument, Nwankwo explains that:

> *The poor technological base of most of the present day African states which has been responsible for their underdevelopment stems from their poor foundation of education laid by the colonialists. Colonial education essentially aimed at training clerks, interpreters, produce inspectors, artisans etc. which would help them in the exploitation[40]of the Africa's rich resources. Colonial education did not aim at industrialization of African territories nor stimulating technological development within the African environment. Colonial education brought about distortion and disarticulation in African indigenous pattern of education which was rooted in African technology…. The introduction of colonial education made Africans to abandon their indigenous technological skills and education in preference to one which mainly emphasizes reading and writing…As we all know, education that is not deeply rooted in a people's culture and environment cannot bring about any meaningful technological advancement. This has aptly been shown in the unsuccessful attempt at the so-called technological transfer, which is more of a myth than a reality.*[41]

---

39 Ibid.
40 Emphasis are mine.
41 Nwankwo, *Colonialism and its Impact in Africa,* 44.

The correctness of Nwankwo's views cannot be gainsaid. When Asian countries like Japan and China are juxtaposed with African countries, it becomes evident that those Asian nations had to shut out Western intervention to achieve proper progress. Although It is apparent that these Asian nations at the annals of industrial development had to shut the door of their relationship with the West. Although Japan at a point had to send people to the West to study their educational and technological systems, the Japanese never jettisoned their indigenous education. They merged the two systems to suit their environment. Today, Japan is one of the most industrialized countries of the world. China similarly, during Mao Zedong's administration in the 1940s and 50s, was moved to ban its nationals from marrying westerners. Consequently, the country advanced to become an industrial giant. Those feats of Asian nations were due to their utilizing their native ingenuity, which the colonizers made Africans discard.

Furthermore, the gains of the United States of America from casting off European interference cannot be exaggerated. Centuries ago, the United States fought off European political might. She evolved her own English, which became contemporary American English. Having achieved autonomy, America assumed the confidence to fully operate international relationships. On the other hand, African products of colonial education have figuratively remained children with milk teeth in the arena of international relations. Africa might be marooned in its undeveloped state unless she frees herself from the shackles of the 'outside world,' just as the United States took its place on the international arena when she was able to subdue European interference.

Another factor that cannot be overemphasized is the impact of Western education on the cultural tenets of

Africans, and the elites created by that instruction. As has been mentioned, Western education initially operated to train interpreters, clerks, messengers and such workers. That was the manifestation of what Lord Lugard termed "The Mission to Civilize[42]". It was summarized by Njoku:

> *The aim in all these was to produce a colonial people, especially the elites, who would be enamored of the ways of western people and desirous to imitate them.* [43]

By the time the colonialists left in the 1960s, they had achieved their overall goal. Africans were left with a bastardized education system. Africans, since then, have been unable to boast of their original intellectualism, nor can they be considered "Europeanized in the real sense of Europe." A scholar has described the impact of western education on the lives of Africans, particularly over language where some of us assume a certain intonation: "a locally Acquired Foreign Accent (LAFA)."[44]

This cultural erosion caused by western education affects other aspects of African culture than language. The *iwa-akwa* ceremony in Igboland might be mentioned. It was an important rite of manhood. Under the influence of Western education, youngsters began to see that essential ceremony as unimportant in determining their social status in traditional

---

42 KorieChima, *Africa and the Wider World*, Lecture delivered to third year students of History and International Studies of University of Nigeria, Nsukka, February, 2015.

43 OnwukaNjoku, *Economic History of Nigeria, 19th -21st Centuries* (second edition) (Nsukka: Grea AP Express Publishers Ltd, 2014) 212.

44 ChidiUgwu, *Indigenous Stranger: The Social Psychology of the Perception and Application of Culture in Nigeria*, C. KrydzIkwuemesi (ed.), Astride Memory and Desire: Peoples, Culture and Development in Nigerian (Enugu:ABIC Books, 2012), 52.

society. Some saw the acquisition of a certificate in the sphere of western education certificate as the ultimate badge of fitness for life. This reached a stage were some refused to undergo the rite of manhood (*iwa-akwa*) until they had completed their formal Western education.

Dear Sibling, from the foregoing, can you now understand that colonialism has succeeded in making us slaves and puppets in the hands of the Pink people? This kind of slavery is a *forever* kind: eternal, endless. It has defined who we are and what we are meant to be, defined our destiny, and defined our colour. Consequently, we are 'black' people.

Sibling, we shouldn't reject ourselves because the West has rejected us. In this exercise of chronicled analyses of our slavery, I would wish you to share my conviction that an unified rejection of our blackness should be our priority. This is designated *Negritude* in literary theory. That concept was popularized by Leopold Senghor. In his essay, '*La Negritude et son expression litteraire,*' Liyan Kesteloot defined *Negritude* as "The simple recognition of the fact of being black, the acceptance of this fact, of our destiny as black people, of our history, and our culture."

Dear Sibling, colonialism was the chief reason why these Pink folks succeeded in making us slaves. We became objects of labour, sent to various countries to work on their farmlands and boost their economies. The brutality we suffered from those masters can't be described. I still hold that the British owe Africans a strong apology for the dehumanization wreaked on us over those years of servitude. Writing those tales infuriates and makes me weep. Is there any better cause for sadness than knowing you are a slave, and need others' validation before you can be heard? Today, for instance, we need the Pink people's validation before we can proclaim someone the oldest person on earth. They simply 'identify' such people without requesting our data. We have in our villages, old men and women who are as old as a hundred and twenty. The Pink people would declare a person of a hundred and five the oldest in the world. We readily accept their pronouncement, because they are the masters and we are the slaves.

My dear Sibling, we lost totally the spirit to resist being slaves and puppets in the hands of the Pink powers. We lost, although we may have fought bravely.

It is true that Africans fought against colonization and failed. However, what happened to Africa subsequently, especially now in the 21st Century? We have accepted defeat. We thank the gods for bringing the Pink people into our land. We go about with homilies, telling the whole world how we would have remained in darkness if the Pink man had not rushed to our rescue. We, the 21st century Africans, might not consider ourselves slaves of the Pink people, yet we zealously ape whatever they do. We now speak the Pink people's language; worship the Pink people's god, dance to the Pink man's music, and even dress like the Pink man. In addition to all that, we dug a deep hole where we buried our own beliefs and cultures, simply because the Pink people have condemned them as 'fetish.'

I shall expound all these in the following chapters. You would ultimately be convinced that we Africans remain slaves and puppets in the hands of Pink people.

THREE

ON CAPITALISM

How would you feel if you discovered that someone gave you a counterfeit of what they are using? How do you feel when you know that what effects progress in other people's homes has a deleterious and retrogressive impact in your own home? Are you lost at what I am saying here? I am talking about *Capitalism.* Do you know how it works in both the Pink man's and Blackman's worlds?

> *It is an economic system in which private individuals and business firms carry on the production and exchange of goods and services through a complex network of prices and markets. Although rooted in antiquity, capitalism is primarily European in its origins; it evolved through a number of stages, reaching its zenith in the 19th century. From Europe, and especially from England, capitalism spread throughout the world, largely unchallenged as the dominant economic and social system until World War I (1914-1918) ushered in modern communism (or Marxism) as a vigorous and hostile competing system.* [45]

---

45 Peterson, Wallace C. "Capitalism." Microsoft® Encarta® 2009 [DVD]. Redmond, WA: Microsoft Corporation, 2008.

Capitalism is an old economic order. Pink people who are the progenitors of this economic system 'invented' it because it suited perfectly their cultural environment, and so on.

At this juncture, I wish to add that this system creates 'a market race.' This implies that Europeans had the need to extend their capitalist ideology to the Black man's world. Out of their ruse-coated mindset, they brought us the counterfeit of capitalism; a mindset intent on using the economic system that favored them to enslave us. We could not discuss how the Pink made us slaves without appraising capitalism. Capitalism would not have been possible but for slavery. The capitalist ideology they gave us – and slavery – became like two sides of a coin. The difference is that the former is based on a forced labour while latter is based on free labour. It was also exploitative. The exploitation was vile. This could be grasped from Samir Amin's response in an interview with L'Humanite:

> "Capitalism has been colonial, more precisely imperialist, during all the most notable periods of its development. The conquest of the Americas by the Spaniards and Portuguese in the 16th century, then by the French and the British, was the first modern form of imperialism and colonization: an extremely brutal form which resulted in the genocide of the Indians of North America, Indian societies in Latin America thrown into slavery and black slavery through the whole continent, North and South... During all the stages of capitalism, the plunder of the resources of the peripheries, the oppression of colonized peoples, their direct or indirect exploitation by capital remains the common characteristics of the phenomenon of colonialism."

It has been clearly stated that while the capitalism brought to Africa was a sham, what's observed in the Pink people's countries comes across as the genuine form. This chapter then proceeds to present a broad outline of how Africans, who were made capitalist slaves, built the edifices Pink people are enjoying today. We shall also examine how the so-called capitalism has failed Africans. First of all, I will show the positive results of this economic ideology in the West, made possible by Africans. Then, we shall survey the contrasting results in Africa.

The glory of the United States was built by slaves. America was built into a strong and formidable nation today with the sweat of slaves on tobacco and cotton plantations. Danielle Young, in her essay titled *"6 Historic Structures in America That Were Built By Slaves,"* published in *The Root* on July 26, 2016, surveyed the six powerful US structures built by slaves during the Trans-Atlantic Slave Trade. The buildings were the US Capitol Building, Railways, Thomas Jefferson's Estate at Monticello, and Buildings at UNC-Chapel Hill, The Wall Street, and the Pink House.

It is no longer news that the Africans whom capitalism transported to the West were central to the establishment of the industries that dominated the western economy. Let me give you a practical example with Wall Street.

Wikipedia states that the "Wall Street is a 0.7-mile-long (1.1 km) street running eight blocks, roughly North-West to South-East, from Broadway to South Street on the East River in the Financial District of Lower Manhattan, New York City. Anchored by Wall Street, New York City has been called both the most economically powerful city and the leading financial center of the world, and the city is home to the world's two largest stock exchanges by total market capitalization, the New

York Stock Exchange and NASDAQ. Several other major exchanges have or had headquarters in the Wall Street area, including the New York Mercantile Exchange, the New York Board of Trade, and the former American Stock Exchange."

The Wall Street described here was founded by slavery. Records have it that African slaves built the very walls that gave Wall Street its name.

Furthermore, the CEO of Berkshire Hathaway, Warren Buffet was the richest billionaire in America. His company was a textile manufacturing firm and he was a slavery profiteer. The American cotton textile industry was based in England. This company was sustained by slaves who picked cotton in the south.

From previous discussions here, it can't be gainsaid that capitalism was the agent of the Western neocolonial activities in the world. It had penetrated the nooks and crannies of Africa even before the colonial period. To the colonial powers, there was the need for their hegemonic influence to be maintained all over the world. The answer to this economic stronghold of the West is capitalism as it is being dispersed at a very high speed by its sister concept of globalization. In several places in this essay, it has been repeatedly pointed out that one of the paramount, if not the chief propellant, of European colonization of the African continent, was to create markets for her home industries, simultaneously providing raw materials for the said industries. After the massive transfer of African resources as planned by the colonizers, African nations were granted independence, the colonizers having carefully installed pliant leaders in the newly independent nations. Inevitably, the emergent states were faced with economic challenges. In Nigeria, for instance, independence was only seven years old when a civil war broke out, ravaging the country for three years. Although there was an economic boom after the war, thanks to the stooges planted by the former colonial masters, the country failed to utilize that glorious windfall. Consequently, by the 1980s, the economy was in a dismal state.

There was pressure from the watchdogs of capitalist economy to intensify colonial economic subjugation of Nigeria. This was done through Trans-National Corporations and the World Bank.

According to Nwosu, Trans-National Corporations are business ventures whose transactions and management cut across national boundaries. They may enter and operate in any country by adopting different strategies.[46] Chukwu defined Trans-Nationals as "business firms or corporations in which the ownership, management, production, and marketing of a particular type of product/service or line of products/services extend over national boundaries, that is to say, it extends beyond one political and economic community."[47] The World Bank, on the other hand, is the outcome of the Breton Woods Conference of 1944. It is part of the United Nations, charged with granting loans for developmental purposes to member nations of the United Nations. It is important to stress at this point that those two are agents of the capitalist world. Let us briefly discuss them one by one, to assess their impact on African countries.

The World Bank has been described as the agent of the United States and her Western European allies, and

---

46 PetermaryNwosu, *Transnational Corporations (TNCs) and Third World Security and Defence,* ,African *Politics*: eds. Emezi C.E and Ndoh C.A., Owerri: Achugo Publications 1998)239.

47 Kabiri, Kenneth Chukwu, *Transnational Corporations and African Nations,* African *Politics*: eds. Emezi C.E and Ndoh C.A., Owerri: Achugo Publications 1998), 283.

a tool for the continuing impoverishment of third world countries. Ndoh and Ngoka have pointed out that the Bank has, since inception, had American citizens as presidents. Notwithstanding the fact that the Bank is meant to grant loans to any member nation that needs them, it should be noted that the United States and her allies dictate who is eligible. To them, loyal countries are deemed eligible. Regarding this, Ndoh *et al.,* write that:

> *During the formative years of the Bank, her proposed loans to Poland and Czechoslovakia were stopped due to U.S. insistence that she would vote against such if presented to the Executive Board. Secondly, a proposed loan to build the Aswan Dam in Egypt was suspended when U.S. Secretary of State, John Foster Dules, decided against it. The bank also stopped lending to Chile during the Allende regime for protest against Allende's nationalization of some American multinational corporations engaged in mining. Others affected by U.S.A. actions included Afghanistan and Vietnam in 1979.[48]*

The World Bank is nothing but a tool to determine who should 'progress' and who should stagnate or be marooned in poverty on the global economic plane. To elucidate this propensity of the World Bank's along with its capitalist bent, Ndoh *et al.* continued: "The bank refused to lend money to countries that are presumed or perceived socialist-oriented such as Chile under Allende, Indonesia under Surkano, but resumed lending

---

48 Paul Abii-Ndoh and P.C.Ngoka,*The World Bank and the Third World,* African *Politics*: eds. Emezi C.E and Ndoh C.A., Owerri: Achugo Publications 1998) 154.

to these countries when rightist regimes came into power.[49] Apart from using it as her capitalist vehicle, the Bank has been used by the same West to catalyze bad leadership in Africa and beyond. A few examples should suffice: her loans to Belgian Congo during the colonial administration, Mobutu's Zaire and Doe's Liberia. The statement of a one-time Secretary of the United States appears indisputable:

> *These banks and other institutions are essentially to America's strategic interest around the world and should continue to receive U.S. support…we have to do something for those countries whose mind we have to capture and those social structures we are trying to preserve…if the U.S ceases its support, the system of international cooperation particularly among the Western powers could begin to unravel, the Soviet Union would become the major beneficiary.[50]*

Apart from the fact that the Bank selects who gets what from it, it also dictates who spends and how the borrowed money is spent. The U.S does this through Transnational Corporations. Cheryl Payers, as quoted by Ndoh *et al.,* has examined the Bank and expressed concern about its lack of sincerity. He frowned upon the Bank's role in promoting the interests of capitalists and international capitalism. Cheryl, according to Ndoh *et al.,* listed the ten ways in which the Bank has continued to impose capitalism, thereby impoverishing the countries meant to be its beneficiaries:

---

49 Ibid, 154.
50 Ibid, 155.

1. By directly helping multinational corporations especially those engaged in mining.

2. Insistence on production for export, invariably benefitting those who control international trade.

3. Discriminating and refusing to give loans to governments that shun international debts acquired fraudulently or those that nationalize exploitative foreign investments.

4. Opposition to protection for infant, locally-owned industries.

5. Finance of projects that entail the denial of control of basic resources such as land, forest, water, etc. by poor people, but beneficial to middlemen and local agents and their international colleagues.

6. Opposition to minimum wage laws, trade union activities and other forces that tend to increase the share of labour in the national income.

7. Insisting on procurement through the international competitive bidding method that favors the largesse of multinationals.

8. Putting pressure on the borrowing countries to improve the legal privileges of the tax liabilities of foreign investment.

9. Opening up of remote regions through transport and telecommunications, thus destroying the natural protection enjoyed by the region.

10. By acting as intermediary for the flow of fund, with tax payers' money got from its developed member countries that serves as guarantee to the safety of bonds it sells.[51]

---

51   Paul Abii-Ndoh et al., *The World Bank and the Third World*, 152-3.

The implementation of the listed ten points by any borrowing nation would undoubtedly hamper the development of that nation. African countries that approach the World Bank and its agencies for succor are figuratively honoring the 'devil's invitation'. This is one of the problems faced till date by countries like Nigeria which, in the closing decades of the 20th century, welcomed the Structural Adjustment Program.

African countries emerged from colonial hegemony in 1957-1975, with the exception of South Africa which was freed from the apartheid regime in the last decade of the 20th century. Forces of underdevelopment, carefully devised by the colonizers before they left, pervaded the entire continent. Thus, debate about Africa's developmental direction was resumed at the end of the 1970s. This occurred after the continent's fragile economies had been rattled by the shock waves of expensive petroleum and industrial decline.[52] Within this time, there was a growing awareness among Africa's leading thinkers that the problem was not merely cyclical and short-term, but structural and long-term as had been deviously designed decades earlier. Then was roused a determination to turn adversity into advantage, to move from enforced to determined self-reliance.[53]

Consequently, there was a "need" by some African countries to borrow money from the International Monetary Fund to balance their trades. The IMF and the World Bank usually impose certain conditions for loans, requiring of borrowers what are called Structural Adjustment Programs.[54]

---

52 ChikeluOfoebe, The Development Process in Africa: The Taxonomy of a Continental Phenomenon: African Politics, ed. Emezi, C.E and Ndoh, C.A. (Owerri: Achugo Publication, 1998), 87.

53 ChikeluOfoebe, ed. Emezi, C.E and Ndoh, C.A. 1998.

54 Tabb, William K. "Globalization." Microsoft® Student 2009 [DVD]. Redmond, WA: Microsoft Corporation, 2008.

This process stipulates what borrowers are expected to do within their countries to stabilize their economy. The conditions include privatization, deregulation, liberalization, and other acts. In summary, borrowers are expected to reconstruct their economies to accord with the dictates of the capitalist system.

The conditions embodied in the Structural Adjustment Program of the International Monetary Fund, impelled some scholars to opine that accepting the IMF /World Bank SAP by African countries was tantamount to honoring the devil's invitation.

The Structural Adjustment Program has been objected to as incapable of solving Africa's problems. T.M Shaw argued that "SAP is unfortunate and unworkable because it reinforces Africa's colonial divisions and retards any prospect for regional cooperation…"[55] He further contended that the Program had failed to provide a solution to the debt crisis in Africa.

Furthermore, it was argued that borrower countries' socio-economic spheres suffered setbacks. Bids to promote education, vocational training facilities and medical services, were all cosmetic and failed. It was also observed that with the rationalization and streamlining of state institutions and enterprises, many jobs were cut off, thus creating unemployment. S. Amin, assessing the social disaster caused by the program, writes: "the social disasters produced by the adjustment programs are not the result of marginal errors which can be corrected by so-called 'Adjustment with a human face, or reintegrating the social dimension in the programs, etc.' They are the logic and necessary consequences of what is wanted."

---

55   ChikeluOfoebe, ed. Emezi, C.E and Ndoh, C.A. 1998. 96.

Having examined the Structural Adjustment Program critically, a scholar categorically declared: "SAP has failed in this country (Nigeria). There is no question about that."[56] This is a fact because hardly has a country that borrowed from the World Bank and its sister agent the – International Monetary Fund – survived it. Nigeria is a typical example. The fluctuation of naira per dollar since the IMF days persists till date.

Capitalism, as pointed out above, also uses Trans-National Corporations to achieve the remaining missions of the West in Africa. This is so because the operations of those corporations, according to Chukwu, are channeled towards exploiting economically buoyant countries. Without doubt, the activities of those companies have marred the security of "Third-World" nations, most of which are African. Security, as mentioned above, was expounded by Subrahmanyam, an Indian economic expert. He held that security "does not mean merely safeguarding of territorial boundaries; it means also ensuring that the country is industrialized rapidly and develops into a cohesive, egalitarian, technological society."[57] It cannot be over-emphasized that these trans-nationals, which are agents of capitalism, have violated Westphalian principles... This is so because the developing countries now serve as dumping grounds for all those corporations.

Similarly, as noted above, security cannot be complete without economic viability. The creation of polar division of labour by colonialism is still evident today. The industries pioneered by those trans-nationals in developing countries of

---

56 ChikeluOfoebe, ed. Emezi, C.E and Ndoh, C.A. 1998.
57 Subrahmanyam, *Our National Security*" quoted in in Peter Nwosu, *Transnational Corporations (TNCs) and Third World Security Defence: African Politics*: eds. Emezi C.E and Ndoh C.A., Owerri: Achugo Publications 1998)240.

Africa cannot, from the available raw materials, process goods to the finished state needed by the populace. Consequently, rather than foster industrialization, trans-nationals have made Third-World countries believe that all their needs should be imported. The situation is so grievous that Nigeria, although abounding in human and natural resources, imports almost everything. Nigeria exports crude oil only to import refined oil! She exports wood only to import toothpicks and pencils!

FOUR

ON CULTURE

There is no better way to define culture than to call it 'the people's way of life.' It is the centrality of how a people carry out their lives and affairs. This goes a long way in representing them and showing their identity. Ejikeme observes that:

> The word culture is most commonly used in three basic senses: excellence of taste in fine arts and humanities; an integrated pattern of human knowledge, belief, and behavior that depends upon the capacity for symbolic thought; and social learning, shared attitudes, values, goals, and practices.[58]

By incorporating social learning in the above description, one might conclude that culture involves everything done in the way humans interact with one another. Shared attitudes

---

58 Joy Ejikeme, *Marketing Nigerian Cultural Heritage: A Boon to National Development* C. KrydzIkwuemesi (ed.), Astride Memory and Desire: Peoples, Culture and Development in Nigerian (Enugu: ABIC Books, 2012),, 137.

specify what then become the dos and don'ts of the society in question. This might be what Ferraro, Trevathan and Levy meant when, in 1994, they defined culture as "what people have, think, and do as members of a society."[59] This is to say that a people can be differentiated from another through their cultural practices. Nigerians too embrace this purview on culture, thus, the cultural policy for Nigeria in 1988 defined it as

> *The totality of way of life evolved by a people in their attempt to meet the challenges of living in their environment, which gives order and meaning to their social, political, economic, aesthetic and religious norms and modes of organization, thus distinguishing a people from their neighbors.*[60]

Similarly, Edward Taylor in 1871 defines culture as:

> *That complex whole which includes knowledge, belief, art, morals, laws, custom, and other capabilities and habits acquired by man as a member of a society.*[61]

All the definitions given above have one common denominator. It is the fact that culture is what defines a given people and differentiates each from the other. As such, any people who lost their cultural heritage as described above, lack identity and as such, live lives that are not worth living.

Now, let us see how Europeans assailed and trampled African culture into worthlessness. Our history and our

---

59 ChidiUgwu, *Indigenous Stranger*, 52.

60 Joy Ejikeme, *Marketing Nigerian Cultural Heritage,* 137.

61 ChidiUgwu, *Indigenous Stranger,* 52.

culture are like two sides of a coin; we cannot do without either. However, as we were slaves to colonialism, we were left with no option but to let our culture be eroded. The African culture has not only failed, it failed woefully. Show me any part of the African nation with a culture that we can be proud of. The truth is that external oppression made our cultures fail, and to replace them, we adopted the cultures of our colonial masters. Thus, we are slaves and our cultural life was life was short-lived. Here is the issue: Africans suffered so much emotional trauma during the slave trade, which weakened us and blighted our cultural life. That situation enabled other cultural values to overwhelm us.

Slaves who were sent to Europe and America, were left with no other option but to adopt the cultures imposed on them, jettisoning theirs. That is why the community is crucial in the preservation of a people's cultural system. When people are displaced, as witnessed during the slave trade, they adopt new ideas and values. That proved to be the lot of the slaves. In some cases, a new culture could enhance the old, but our reality under colonization was dismal. The change in outlook could occur consciously as well as unconsciously. The conclusion is that people forge new and strange identities when they lose their culture.

Culture holds some of the secrets of life's purpose. No authentic identity exists apart from culture. Most of Africa's inhabitants can't speak of culture without mentioning drums, palm trees and elephants. Funnily, however, those quantities do not comprehensively define the culture of Africa. For instance, those who visit Haiti will encounter voodoo. An Ethiopian might view their culture as emanating from the coffee ritual. Based on the foregoing, it can be concluded that even African culture is not properly defined. How then could an undefined culture be protected? Is it possible to secure an unprotected territory? Should one wait for a people to be dead or effaced before a culture is preserved? Is it not fact that people's culture has relevance only when the people are living?

Although Africa comprises many nations, most of Africa's cultures are communal. Implicit in that communalism are adherent to ethics and respect for human rights. This observation contradicts the notion that African cultures reflect national homogeneity, differing from one country to another. It is true to assert that what truly define us as Africans are our cultural lives. Should we discard them, the result would be disastrous: because religion, music, aesthetics, family formations, marriage rites and other rites and practices cannot be detached from culture.

Africans believed that at some stage in life, youths must start to assume responsibility for their lives. Our ancestors devised ceremonies to launch youths into adult membership of society. They created what we call *rites of passage* today.

My fellow African people, I have encountered many Africans who told me that colonization and civilization did us good, citing technological developments. Personally, I believe that those developments are all manifestations of modernism, and modernism does not reflect degrees of civilization. It is possible for an "uncivilized" society to brandish the latest weapons of war. Should we then hold that because a nation possesses those technological devices, it is civilized? The answer, my brothers and sisters, is no.

Culture, by its nature, tends to interact with whatever comes across it, including modernity. As Africans, we are impacted by prevalent modernities, which are not necessarily Pink or West. They are products of global human effort.

Culture is instilled into people's lives and limbs by

constant acts of repitition. A culture that is not practiced, adhered to and maintained withers and dies. A people that abandoned their culture have never been known to prosper. The crisis of African people is perhaps attributable to their abandonment of their culture for the Pink people's. Our culture can still exist even in the midst of modernity. Rite of passage can still be preserved, whether they are 'civilized' or not. Payment of bride price have always been part of our core values, and should be respected.

So completely have we lost every sense of our Africanness that we now prefer European paintings to the African arts at our doorsteps. Consequently, African arts are dying. Even African artists are now painting pictures of the West to fulfill the demands of their African patrons and collectors!

I praise – and will forever laud – Thomas Sankara. When Sankara assumed power, he declared locally produced cotton Burkina Faso's national fabric, and instructed all civil servants to start wearing it. This gave a commercial boost to the indigenous clothing industry, and promoted pride in African apparel. I have travelled to various African countries, and on many occasions argued with their hotel managements for not offering African cuisine. They give no reasons for that deficiency: it is simply not trendy to serve African fare. I now repeat what I have stated in many places: "The problem with us Africans is mental slavery." Ask questions, and when you are provided with true answers, you will then understand that most Africans despise their cultures, because they consider those cultures backward, ancient or embarrassing. How do Africans build their houses today? In the past, architects created their own designs which resulted in beautiful and authentic structures. Today, houses built in that mode are almost extinct. Our architects work in accordance with European concepts and designs, without knowing they are hastening the collapse of our culture.

We need to make our culture powerful. We must accomplish that, or else be consigned to eternal slavery. Many would agree that, with the westernization that pervades this continent, African products are almost universally disdained. Artistically pleasing hand-made chairs are now replaced with plastic furniture imported from China. The foreign imports of course enhance the economies of the foreign countries, which continue to facilitate their dominance of our nations. My dearest Sibling…, Europeans made us cultural slaves, and we began to adore and ape whatever they did. We began to take Pink names, speak their language, dress in their outfits, accepting inferiority.

Africans need to understand themselves and unite. We can't achieve anything without unity. If we fail in this, our marginalization by Western powers will not end. We must also ensure that we retain our fundamental ethos. The following chapters will examine some aspects of culture that have been bastardized, resulting into further enslavement.

FIVE

ON LANGUAGE

A s you read and ponder the following paragraphs, ask yourself in what language you think. In what medium and sphere of meaning are you processing the thoughts and ideas being communicated? The language of your thoughts determines the depth of your psychological connection to the material being studied. I think in Igbo, my native language, and not in English or French. I understand that language is as strong as a people and their everyday lives.

For a people's culture to be what it ought to be, it must have a mode of expression. This device or vehicle is the language of the said people. Language is indispensable to cultural discourse because without it, culture could not be disseminated. Everything one does, from thinking to interpreting, is defined by language. The compelling conclusion is that the loss of a people's language is the loss of the foundation of their culture. I will always think in the Igbo language. Consequently, my behavior must reflect the Igbo language.

One can declare that Africa's cultural practices, ingenuity and technology are swiftly ebbing away, because of the loss of her lingua linkages. A thorough scrutiny of the educational sectors of African countries would substantiate this contention. The situation in other parts of the world is different. Ugwu alludes to a statement of Aniekon's, of a Japanese undergraduate saying: "When my father was an undergraduate, he took his lecture notes in both English and Japanese. In my generation, we took our lecture notes in Japanese."[62] I would infer that this is one of the secrets of Japan's present scientific and technological excellence, which I've already alluded to. The Japanese government realized that language was the carrier of a people's culture, as a people can only attain their best when they act in cognizance of their environment. This was not so in Africa. Many Africans regard their native languages as irrelevant and backwards, and feel they should simply be allowed to die. Many Nigerian parents pride themselves in raising children who are more fluent in English than their native tongue.

As long as people's culture exists, language is crucial. Nothing can be done without language. Lamentably, many African languages have become extinct because of the presence and deeds of the Pink people; they impressed on us that our mother tongues were irrelevant, and we strove to be 'progressive' and 'trendy.' This chapter aims to highlight the evil effects of this propensity, and why Africans will remain slaves as long as we "speak with our noses."

Europeans did not even learn the languages of the people they came to plunder. Of course, we lived before they came, and considered us lesser animals. In their view we merely existed, and they discarded much that was indigenous in our culture. Rather than learn our languages, which they should have considered their primary task, they sought interpreters. Even in the present, Africans are delighted when some

---

62 ChidiUgwu, *Indigenous Strangers,* 57.

unintelligent Pink person who wouldn't take the trouble to learn our language, begins to bastardize it. Have we ever asked ourselves how they react when we sing in English?

Language is the basis of our being and existence. Self-denial and self-abnegation are the African man's biggest problems. He denies everything about himself: his culture, his language, his identity, his weakness and, sometimes, himself. An African man would tell himself a lie and begin to believe his own lies. When you continually believe in your own falsehood, you are in the throes of self-deception. You have a problem you may never be able to solve.

The coming of Pink people, with their introduction of Indo-European languages as the official languages of the colonized countries, killed African languages. African peoples were taught to speak those languages. All that mattered were addressed in the languages of the lords and masters, while their own tongues were suppressed or effaced. What many don't seem to realize is that a lost language is a lost culture. Many African children can no longer speak their indigenous languages. In many African homes, parents forbid their children to speak native African languages. Ugwu, obviously embittered by the faults of a typical Igbo parent, writes:

> ...many parents now get angry at anybody who speaks their local language to their children. They always retort, "Don't speak that **thing**[63] to my child". On occasions where the children meet with their grandparents, their parents tell them, "Say hi to Grandma/Grandpa" who are always at a loss as to how to respond. When confronted with the dangers of this, such parents present the excuse that since lessons at school are conducted in

---

63 Emphasis is mine.

English, it would do their children a good turn if they get used to it from home.[64]

Consequently, an average Igbo child who lives in the urban area would be proud to say, "I do not understand the Igbo language." The belief is that the more one rids oneself of the Igbo language, the more "modern and classy" one becomes. The end achieved is always the opposite of what is desired. Those deluded people end up being neither authentically African like their forbears, nor European like the Europeans. This is a contributory factor to Africa's backwardness. Even with the English language we have embraced, it is hardly possible for one to speak the language of another cultural group with the fluency, intonation and speed of the original owners of the language. There tend to be disparities of fluency between a second user of a language and a native speaker. If anything, there is the phonological interference from a second user's mother-tongue, notwithstanding the Locally Acquired Foreign Accent paraded today. What is worse is that sometimes we prefer Pidgin English, otherwise called *"Broken"* to our indigenous languages.

This trend persists among African youth who should engineer the continent's new cultural direction. I meet many young Igbo people who proudly tell me they can't speak Igbo when I try to converse in the language. I always remind them that language is not just a means of communication, but also an identity marker. It serves as a symbol for people who belong to the same ethnic group, and who share a common heritage.

My dear Sibling, language influences even our perception of our environment. Consequently, it determines the extent to which we can safeguard and retain the knowledge and wisdom

---

64 Ibid, 57.

passed down through generations. Ethnologists record that there are 2,138 living languages spoken by Africa's population of over 1 billion. Nigeria alone leads in the number of languages spoken with 526 languages.

In Nigeria, the prominent languages are Hausa, Igbo, Yoruba and Pidgin, in addition to English, which became the official language after Pink men enslaved us. The other 522 languages are dying, as the native speakers move to urban areas and fail to teach their children their native tongues. If Nigeria spoke her 526 languages, we would have about 342,205 speakers per language. This calculation is based on the country's population of over 170 million. Cameroon follows Nigeria with about 281 languages spoken by its 22.5 million people. If they spoke their languages as they should, they would have at least 80,194 speakers of each language. However, they are not speaking their languages; they adhere to the languages of their colonial masters.

You may be wondering if there is anything wrong with the death of a language, but that demise has more consequences than many realize. When a language is lost, the wealth of culture and history of a people dies with it. Language is the reservoir of culture, wealth, philosophy, history and even medicinal practices.

Linguists have noted that languages are critically endangered, and have continued to disappear through the assimilation of bigger languages. All Africans should be concerned and alarmed about this.

Language can simply be endangered when there are very few speakers, and its use is continually diminished. Many African languages are disappearing because of countries' policies on language. Many of course consider it prestigious to speak English and degrading to speak their indigenous languages. This attitude pervades East, West and Southern Africa. Similar glamourizing of the French language and scorn of native languages occur in francophone countries.

According to statistics released by UNESCO, there are 231 extinct languages in the world and 37 of those are languages of Sub-Saharan Africa. The Zeem language in Nigeria, the Berakou in Chad, Kwadi in Angola, and Kw'adza in Tanzania are among the dying ones.

Now, a survey of some African countries will reveal that our African languages are dying without any hope of resuscitation. As stated earlier, Ethnologists list Nigeria as having 15 dying languages. UNESCO classifies 14 as critically endangered and among them is the Yangkam language, which in 1996 had only 100 speakers. Of course the number decreases every year. Even most speakers of Yangkam have begun to speak Hausa, although they maintain their Bashar identity. Reflecting on the decline recorded in 1996, there is no accurate record of how many speakers survive today.

In Cameroon, the Bikya and Bishuo were listed as having only one speaker each in 1986. In Central Africa, Birri, Bodo, and Geme languages were noted as endangered. The Bodo, a language spoken by the Bantu people, had only 15 speakers in 1996. In that year, the Birri language had 200 speakers left while the Geme had 500. In Chad, the Berakou, Nov, Massalat, Buso, Mabire, and Goundo languages are endangered, while the fate of an Ethiopian language is grievous, as it had only eight speakers in 2007. The speakers evince no zeal to preserve the languages, and do not strive to pass them to younger people. Somalia has about 13 languages, and one called Boon is nearly extinct. In South Africa, three languages are on the brink of total extinction: the Korana, Xiri, and the Nlu. In 2013, there were only 3 speakers of the Nlu left. Kenya faces a similar fate, for three of its languages are almost extinct. They are the Yaaku, the Elmolo, and the Omotik. The people of Elmono live on the shore of Lake Turkana in the country's North West. As at 1994, there were only 8 speakers of the language left.

The Mukogodo was spoken by a hunter-gathered group that settled in the Mukogodo forest of Kenya. They lost their language in the 1930s.

We Africans have not done much to avert the death of our languages. Like slaves, we believe those indigenous tongues are unimportant and shamelessly extol the languages our colonial masters foisted on us. The extinction of our languages will mar our economic, social and political lives. Although we accept that life is dynamic, it should not result in our abjuring our indigenous tongues. If we did so, we would lose our identities. Lamentably, many of those endangered languages will not survive the 21st century.

SIX

ON RELIGION

I am going to present religion to you in its purest form as it was brought and planted by Pink people. I intend to be plain, as I would not want you to be misled. Furthermore, I shall be blunt without minding whose susceptibilities are wounded.

I would like to start with a few questions: Can you define religion? Did you know that Africans had viable religions before Pink people introduced and imposed theirs on us? Did you know that the emergent Pink people's religion is not without deceptions? Do you know that religion that is not constructed in line with a people's culture is bound to retard their development? Did you know that the emergent religious groups in Africa are major sources of our under-development? If your answer to any of these is NO, calm down and remain focused. We are on an expository exploration that should provide answers to those questions.

We shall define religion. Note, however, that scholars have struggled and foundered over finding a universally accepted definition of religion. This is because, among other factors, religion as a concept evokes emotional feelings as well as physical and metaphysical beings.[65] Thus, there is no one acceptable definition. The World Encyclopedia as quoted in Anyanwu defines it as man's attempt to achieve the best by allying himself with the highest power.[66] I would add that religion is the aspect of a people's cultural practices that relates to physical and metaphysical beings.

I am often angered when people say that Europeans brought the African man spirituality. We Africans were very spiritual people even before the Pink man came to our land. We "did our own things" happily – danced when we should, sang when we should, and fought, if necessary. This lifestyle was observed and related by the young slave, Olaudah Equiano, as far back as the 18th Century AD, when he described Igboland as a "nation of dancers, musicians, and poets". He further said that every great event such as a triumphant return from battle, or other causes of public rejoicing, was celebrated with songs and music suited for the occasion.[67]

This shows that before the advent of Pink people, Africa had her religious practices. One single term, 'African Traditional Religion,' has been used to describe it. Drawing an analogy with Igboland, the people worshipped one Supreme God, though the mode of doing this varied from place to place.

In some places, he gets no more than occasional invocations of his name during some critical acts and

---

65 Anyanwu Timothy, A Study of the Ethno-Religious Conflicts in Nigeria's Political System, 1960-1999, An unpublished M.Sc. Project. Peace Studies and Conflict Resolution Department, National Open University of Nigeria, July, 2017.

66 Encyclopedia, in Anyanwu Timothy.

67 Paul Edwards (eds.), Anyanwu Timothy Chibuike, The Social and Economic Impacts of the Iwa-Akwa Ceremony In Ehime Mbano, Imo State: 1960-2013.Unpublished B.A. Project, Department of History and International Studies, University of Nigeria, Nsukka, July, 2015,4.

prayers. In other places, he receives sacrifices and different forms of offerings.[68]

Irrespective of the mode of worship, however, the whole of Igboland believed that with belief and trust in God, one would obtain one's needs, and that anyone acting contrary to the will of the Supreme God would be punished by Him. This single belief gave them a sense of morality. Although they may not have had a codified law, they were ardent believers of their creed. Social vices were abhorred.

In return, the Supreme God whom they reverenced wholeheartedly provided for them, made their farms flourish, and blessed them with children and all their needs. Flourish they did, until the advent of Western missionaries. Evidence exists from the first Europeans to make contact with a territory in what became Nigeria: Benin and its environs. The empire of Benin was thriving and well organized before the coming of the Pinks. Anene observes thus:

Benin, one of the most remarkable of the states of the Guinea forest, was the centre of an empire the size and orderliness of which attracted the attention of the Portuguese who visited the Guinea coast towards the end of the fifteenth century. These visitors were impressed by the size of the metropolis itself, with its great streets and rows of neat houses...[69]

---

68 ChukwuOgbajie, *The Impact of Christianity on the Igbo Religion and Culture, (Umuahia: Ark Publishers, 1995)*13.

69 J. C. Anene, *The People of Benin, the Niger Delta, Congo and Angola in the Nineteenth Century,* Joseph C. Anene and Godfrey N. Brown eds. *Africa in the Nineteenth and Twentieth Centuries,* (Ibadan: University Press, 1966), 270.

The foregoing shows that Africa was advanced before the arrival of Pink people. If human success should be ascribed to supernatural beings, then Africans throve on the benevolence of their gods whom they worshipped in various forms of African religion.

It might be argued that religion operates beneficially in a community when the said religion is practically contextualized. In other words, the tenets of a particular religion would function well in a community fused with that creed. Instructive is the remark of William Benett's quoted by Ezeh: "When we have disdain for our religious tradition, we have disdain for ourselves."[70] William believes that culture and tradition are the definitions of a people; and religion is an integral part of the said culture. Similarly, Bodley describes culture as:

> *The patterns of behavior and thinking that people living in social groups learn, create, and share. Culture distinguishes one human group from others. It also distinguishes humans from other animals. A people's culture includes their beliefs, rules of behavior, language, rituals, art, and technology, styles of dress, ways of producing and cooking food, **religion**[71], and political and economic systems.*[72]

70 Peter-Jazzy Ezeh, *Religion, Cultural Hegemony and Post-Colonial Social Order in Africa,* C. KrydzIkwuemesi (ed.), Astride Memory and Desire: Peoples, Culture and Development in Nigerian (Enugu:ABIC Books, 2012), 81.

71 Emphasis is mine.

72 Bodley, John H. "Culture." Microsoft® Student 2009 [DVD]. Redmond, WA: Microsoft Corporation, 2008.

Similarly, Muriel Spark observes that "Art and religion first; then philosophy; lastly, science. That is the order of the great subjects of life, that's their order of importance."[73]

Sequel to the foregoing, one can see why Christianity, which was imposed on Africans by the colonizers, is yet to connect with the people because of the loss of the African identity. This view is succinctly summarized in the *Amended Burial as Per-Custom and Tradition of Umuomanwoke,* thus:

> *Tradition is sacred. Custom is above all. To question tradition is sacrilege. If men do not respect tradition, how can our society stand? How can we be proud of our forefathers? And pass on our pride to our children or allowed to change our ancient practices as we like? For us, tradition is not a passing thing. It is the air we breathe and the earth on which we lie. It is what makes us different from other communities.*[74]

Therefore, the coming of the Pink man's religion was a harbinger of changes and challenges in the African religious setting. The effect of this religious group in the traditions of the aboriginals cannot be overemphasized. Now most of our traditional rulers are Christians who are applauded for frequenting the church and Muslims who uphold the Islamic religion. Isn't it disgraceful that people who should be the Faces of their respective cultures are now worshipping the Pink people's God and the Arabic God? Can you, dear Sibling, imagine the Queen of England or a king in any

---

73 Muriel Spark, quoted in Peter-Jazzy Ezeh, *Religion, Cultural Hegemony and Post-Colonial Social Order in Africa,* C. KrydzIkwuemesi (ed.), Astride Memory and Desire: Peoples, Culture and Development in Nigerian (Enugu:ABIC Books, 2012), 81.

74 the Amended Burial as Per-Custom and Tradition of Umuomanwoke

European nation kneeling down in our shrine to worship Amadioha or any other African deity? Of course they cannot, and that is why I will always consider our traditional rulers who worship foreign gods foolish. Foolish, too, is their preference of British and Arabic names over African names. In Igboland, for instance, we have traditional rulers who bear names like Charles, Michael and David, and you tell me that these brainwashed men are the Faces of our Culture? I will perhaps speak of them with respect when I see European kings and queens bearing names like Emeka, Ngozi, Obi or even Onyeka! But this dream seems unrealistic, and that makes me sad for Africa. Religion is so powerful that it has completely captured the mindscape of the African man. I sometimes have the opportunity to speak to young people in Nigeria, and I often ask them: "How did Pink people grab an entire continent and enslave the people into their religion?" I pose this question because I believe religion was the cheapest means by which the Pink man enslaved us. This successful subjugation was aided by the importation of foreign gods into our system. They so brainwashed African parents that even some living today have not cast off their spiritual shackles. In the present age, our parents are ignorant of many important facts. We must not conceal knowledge for fear of hurting their feelings. We must dialogue with them, because change is ceaseless. Many of our parents are left behind in the advance of true enlightenment. They are stuck in their adopted religion, believing that if they failed to pray to the Pink man's god, their problems would not be solved. When they say, "Don't you know that it is because we are praying for you that you are alive today?" ask them, "What about the ones who died?" Ask them, "What about those who lived before the coming of the Pink man and his god?" You might go further to enquire of them why the African continent remains backward, compared to continents whose indigenes are far less prayerful than Africans. Continually ask questions of your parents, unless you are so feckless that you could not care for yourself if they flared up and banished you from their homes. Leave their houses for them if they are unable to accept the truth. Join me to tell them the truth. We have to tell them the truth about this religion that has turned father against mother, brother against sister, and nations against continents, while there is no one to set us free. This religion has destroyed the unity of Africa; it has vanquished Africa. We all know how peaceful our nation used to be. History tells what understanding prevailed among Africans until the bows and arrows of religion intruded to destroy their serenity. The very few people who clung bravely to their indigenous African religions were reviled as "evil" and "pagan," and forced by societal pressure to renounce their creed. Societal pressure was an overwhelming force. The upshot was that Africans turned against one another, identified the Pink man, and fought even their own kin. I weep for you!

I proceed to share a certain experience. In November 2016, I was at Ideal Academy in Washington DC, where I spoke briefly on Igbo mythology, from Ogbuide to Ogbanje in Igbo cosmology, touching slightly on the rituals of *Saraka* and *Uhie* and some small details of Igbo traditional religion. Kevonte Anderson, a certain co-teacher who discoursed upon traditional religion in Yorubaland of Western Nigeria, impressed me. I understood that he knew much about Yoruba deities. Indeed, he knew far more than some of our parents who claim to know, but are dreadfully uninformed. The Igbo of Southeastern Nigeria were quick to embrace Christianity, becoming more Christianized than the Europeans. I have come to tell you, dear Sibling, how religion has fettered us in excruciating slavery. It has made us virtually "blank out," unable to think like the humans we are. We refer to religion before undertaking many tasks.

Thanks to the gods, exceptions exist. Having appraised Christianity's role in the erosion of Igbo religio-cultural values, Afigbo described the Christian mission as "the most thorough-going cultural imperialism of those days, and even today."[75] He further explained:

> *The Christian mission cashed in on these uncritical and unrestrained Igbos longing for European culture to dismantle nearly all the ancient cultural landmarks in Igbo society. So iconoclastic did the missions become that they infuriated many members of the colonial administration by their radical reforms. At one point, Herbert Richmond Palmer, the Lieutenant Governor General of Northern Nigeria, commenting on the affair, said it was the policy of the missions to destroy the fabric of Igbo life in order to build upon the ashes thereof.*[76]

On his own part, Onwuka Njoku, observing the motives of Christian churches, writes:

> *All the Christian churches came to Nigeria with a common but mistaken conviction: that traditional African religion along with African culture was heathen and had to be eradicated, if the people were to benefit from the presumed largesse of western civilization.*[77]

---

75 E.A. Afigbo, *Towards Cultural Revival Amongst the Igbo-Speaking Peoples*, (eds.)UgoAgada and KemjikaAnoka:Anu Magazine, 3., 4.

76 Ibid.

77 Onwuka N. Njoku, *Economic History of Nigeria, 19th -21st Centuries*, (Nsukka, Great AP Express Publishers Ltd, 2014) 212.

With the embrace of this new religious practice, "things started to fall apart" in the lives and other cultural practices of Africans. Anyanwu, for instance, related the influence of two missionaries, Rev. Fathers Walsh and Ho-Well in Agbaghara-Nsu, a community in Eastern Nigeria, over the culture of Iwa-Akwa.[78] This was in the first decades of the 20th Century. Those missionaries greatly changed the conduct of the festival. Anyanwu further noted that although Christianity effected changes in Iwa-akwa, it was considerably conservative compared to events of the 1980s when '**New Generational Churches**[79] sprouted in the region. He averred that the extent of the devaluation of Iwa-akwa in that period could not be exaggerated. The number of participants greatly decreased from the 1980s. In most cases, he further stated, lazy young men who loathed to be industrious like their fellows, avoided the ceremony. Their excuse invariably was that Iwa-akwa was an act of paganism. That ruse of course connoted virtue and piety. It effectively freed them from respecting and undergoing that rite of passage.[80]

Notwithstanding what the Pink man told Africans about his religion, the truth must be told, which is that:

---

78 Iwa-akwa means 'wearing cloth'. It is a ceremony performed by youths especially boys in Igboland, to initiate them into manhood/adulthood in the village. Until this ceremony is performed, the individual is not recognized or referred to as an adult. He is referred to as a boy notwithstanding that he is grown up or rich. He is not invited to any meeting of the elders or adults. He is not expected to make any financial contribution for the development of the village

79 This shows that churches keep emerging in Africa as days pass. The resultant effect is that the continent would continue to be befuddled by religious cobwebs.

80 Anyanwu Timothy Chibuike, The Social and Economic Impacts of the Iwa-Akwa Ceremony In Ehime Mbano, Imo State: 1960-2013. Unpublished B.A. Project, Department of History and International Studies, University of Nigeria, Nsukka, July, 2015, 40.

*He came to Africa with a preconceived idea of the superiority of his race, his religion and the customs and institutions of his country... He encouraged his wards to imitate himself in all respects and gave them the impression that **the less African they were the more Christian they became.**[81]*

The foregoing shows why Africans had to embrace the foreign religion without questions. My fellow Africans, we are in serious slavery and must remain so as long as we remain more Christianized than Christianity itself, and bear the names of Pink people. Yes, we embraced their religion and began to answer the names they gave us. We 'threw away' our native names, thereby throwing ourselves away. Today, we bear so many Christian and Arabic names that it is difficult to identify our kin.

I now share my personal story. I spent 6 years in the seminary, reading the Bible and praying a lot. I later renounced Christianity for my own reasons, some of which I've been expressing in this chapter. I was born a Christian, which was why I grew up a Christian. However, now that I am able to make my own decisions, I make them. I was born "Onyekachukwu George Nwelue," but all my credentials now bear "Onyeka Nwelue," the name I prefer. I went to court and deposed to an affidavit to effect that change. My father helped me inform the Anglican Church of the change, and my name remains as I have made it. Let me state that I draw satisfaction from being African, at least in name.

At this stage, I wish to remind you, and those whom you may show this letter to, that we have lots of work to do on our parents. Most of their errors in the name of religion were

_____

81 Emphasis are mine.

unintentional. They were misled. They were too blind to fault the Christian missionaries who hectored them about their "barbarity," ridiculing polygamy, tattooing, slavery, bride-price, and other cultural practices of theirs. Africans failed to point out that

> *The Christian missionary preached equality of all men before God, but in the church he was frequently the imperious master; he emphasized the spiritual danger of faithful converts laying up for themselves treasures in this world, but at the same time the missionary's 'brothers', traders, concentrated on earthly prosperity, often at the African's expense; the missionary preached against the sinfulness of drunkenness, but the Africans saw themselves being compelled to exchange their oil and elephant teeth mostly for exciting spirits.* [82]

The Africans failed to realize that the missionaries who urged them to drop "superstitious" beliefs, gave them nothing concrete to allay their fears. They failed to ask the missionaries the basis of their teachings. They rather let it all sink into their marrow, resulting in a problem that is evident today.

Apart from the doctrinal harm wreaked on the African world by the missionaries, there were pieces of evidence that they actively instigated violence amongst African communities. Regarding this, Ayandele observes:

> *It is essential to emphasize the fact that in the middle of the nineteenth century, missionaries found chiefs at loggerheads one with the other whether in the small kingdoms of Badagry, Lagos, or Old Calabar,*

---

82 Ibid.

*or in the interior among the tribal groups of Egbas,
Ibadans, Ijebus and Oyos. In Badagry, the Wawu,
chiefs of English Town, and traditionally only fourth
in hierarchy among the chiefs, were already claiming
a constitutional status that traditionally belonged to
Chief Akran, chief of Portuguese Town. And British
traders were already encouraging Wawu's claims. In
Lagos, the dynastic struggle between Akintoye and
Kosoko was already brewing. In the interior, Egbas,
who were surrounded by the enemies – Ibadan, Ijebu
and Dahomey – invited missionaries in order to fulfil
the Egba's political aspiration. They expected that
the missionaries would supply them with weapons of
precision, bestow upon them economic prosperity and
drive away their enemies…the missionaries reduced the
various economic and political issues which concerned
the combatants to purely ethical denominator.[83]*

Most of those African leaders, clinging to the missionaries,
were unaware of the missionaries' intentions. Before reality
dawned on them, it was too late. The chiefs did not know how
and when they lost their lands to the Pink man in exchange
for umbrellas, mirrors, and other European goods that they
wanted rather than needed.

*Take for instance, the pathetic case of Mzilikazi
of Matabeleland and Robert Moffat, of London
Missionary Society Missionary. Both of them became
friends but later the former regretted their friendship
on the grounds that traders and settlers came to seize*

83   Ibid, 137-8.

his lands and sovereignty through Robert Moffats's exertions. It is not surprising then that Mzilikazi's son, Lobengula, described the process of British infiltration into his country to a missionary in 1889 in these words. 'Did you ever see a chameleon catch a fly? The chameleon gets behind the fly and remains motionless for some time, then he advances very slowly and gently, first putting forward one leg and then another. At last, when well within reach, he darts out his tongue and the fly disappears. England is the chameleon and I am the fly'. In Buganda, East Africa, the Kabakas thought they could use missionaries for their own political ends. But as a result, during the scramble, the British Protestant Missionaries consciously worked to see that the country became part of the British Empire, whilst the French Catholic Missionaries also exerted themselves to see that the territories were annexed by any power but the British. What was more; the chiefs and their supporters became divided into pro-British and pro-French factions. Even the Muslims came to be involved in the 'religious wars'… [84]

However, it may be argued that the impact of missionaries in the development of African society is enormous. That may seem true, because apologists hold that missionaries brought western education, health centers, abolished "evil" cultural practices and did other good deeds. However, beside all these seeming truths, we have examined the quality of the education brought by the missionaries as discussed above. Furthermore, in Belgian Congo where the Berlin Act permitted missionaries

---

84   Ibid.139.

of all nationals to thrive, it was evident that the government used missionaries as her malleable agents. The Congo's case was observed and articulated by Ajayi *et al*:

> *Since the state paid the mission pipers it called the curriculum tune. The result was not 'education' in its accepted meaning but rather what would better called 'training'. The protestant missions were not assisted, and elsewhere, the cost of secondary education in quality and quantity proved difficult if not impossible without state aid. The Congo, therefore, with the largest mission establishment in Tropical Africa could not produce an elite before its independence.*[85]

The foregoing has made it glaring that the education brought by the missionaries to African societies was questionable. Similarly, one would be justified to ask why Congo, which had the majority of the missions in tropical Africa, was its least educated country at independence. This irony suffices to take the mask off missionary societies and their education. The more missionaries a colonial community had, the worse its situation. This trend is still evident. Nigeria, despite its thousand and one churches and "men of God," is one of the most corrupt countries in the world.

In the sphere of healthcare provision, it is hard to see what benefits have endured from the early establishment of healthcare in Africa. Taking Nigeria as an example, a country that had health facilities for over a century can now provide its citizens with only epileptic healthcare facilities. Consequently, many affluent Nigerians are flown abroad for treatment when they are indisposed.

---

85   J.F.A. Ajayiet, al, *The Emergence of a New Elite in Africa*, 156.

Of the so called abolition of "evil practices," claimed to have been accomplished by the Pink people, some epistemological cobwebs remain to be cleared. One is tempted to ask: "what is the meaning of 'evil' as used in this context? Who identifies what is evil? By what yardstick are those 'evils' measured?" Except when those and more questions are answered, the credit given to the Pink man's religion in this regard remains contentious.

Without much ado, the coming of external religious groups in Africa created disorder, wars and misunderstanding which ravage the area till date. It wreaked misplaced priorities and lost identity on Africans. It caused a decline in the indigenous African educational system and technological development. The result of these was retardation in various spheres of African existence. The loss of identity by the African man, the belief that every status is for them the devil's, every gathering, a coven; every symbolic figure, a talisman; and every medicine man, a sorcerer.[86]

It is appalling that Africans accepted the psychological disorientation inflicted by Pink people. The notion that everything about African Traditional Religion was satanic was swallowed without questioning. We embraced the European religion without ascertaining the origins of some of those religious practices. The situation was similar even with African Muslims. The African Muslim is glad to go to Mecca as the religious center of Islam, but fails to ask the link between the stone at Ka'aba in Saudi Arabia and the Pre-Islamic religion of the area. After all, they have been taught to impugn their

---

86 ChidiUgwu, *Indigenous Stranger: The Social Psychology of the Perception and Application of Culture in Nigeria*, C. KrydzIkwuemesi (ed.), Astride Memory and Desire: Peoples, Culture and Development in Nigerian (Enugu: ABIC Books, 2012), 55.

own religion, and submit to all the teachings of the foreign one. Naturally, the Christianity spearheaded by Europe had elements of pre-Christian European cultural practice. This point was remarked by Greene and quoted by Ugwu:

> [W]hen Christianity got to Europe, it did not cause them to wipe away everything they had; they rather domesticated it to suit them. The days of the week and months of the year now used in most parts of the world ring with names of the European pre-Christian "pagan" deities. They also made the commemoration of the birth and death of Jesus to happen in the period of their "pagan" festivals celebrating the birth of the sun in December and the conquest of the sun over darkness in March/April. Again few African couples today know that what they did as church wedding, with suits and [Pink] gowns and rings, were European custom that Christianity picked up when it got there.[87]

Among other outstanding facts noted in the foregoing are the days of the week and the Pink wedding, popularly called "white wedding." It is obvious that only very few young Igbo people could name the traditional Igbo weekdays. Those weekdays, named after the four Igbo market days, if not already forgotten, will probably not survive the first half of this century. Regarding the Pink wedding, it has been recalled in this that one of the practices the missionaries instructed Africans to discard was the bride price custom. They termed it evil. Ugwu, in the foregoing quote, makes clear why the Pink people were moved to denounce the bride-price ceremony, termed the "traditional wedding ceremony" or *"Igba Nkwu*

---

87 ibid, 55-6.

Nwanyi" in Igboland. They wanted Africans to embrace the Pink wedding ceremony of which Africans knew little. Unfortunately, they succeeded. In Igboland today, virtually every bride yearns to be wedded in Church as Pink people do. The traditional wedding ceremony is increasingly disregarded or even despised, and its chances of survival are slim. In some parts of Igboland, only couples married in Church are considered deserving of wedding gifts. The traditional wedding is not deemed appropriate for the presentation of gifts. What a pity!

Those, and more religious deceptions, continue to pose insurmountable challenges to the continent. Such drawbacks include – but are not limited to – suspicion, religious plundering and strife, an instance of which is the perennial conflict between Christians and Muslims. The Boko Haram menace ravaging Nigeria for more than a decade is traceable to Western church ideologies. There are doctrinal clashes and condemnation of one another's creeds. Although Nigeria must be among the nations with the highest number of zealous churchgoers, it remains one of the most corrupt countries in existence. I neither bemoan the advent of external religions nor am I against the proliferation of churches. My view is that those developments should be conditioned to suit the people's culture. Africans' xenocentrism should have been rejected for acculturation, as prevailed in the Vietnamese Catholic Mission. Regarding this, Ugwu, quoting the Newsweek of 5th April, 2004, says:

> *A cardinal from Vietnam, Pham Minh Man, was asked what the difference was between a European and a Vietnamese Catholic. His response was simple: "Culture!" After Vatican II, the Vietnamese council*

of bishops had met and approved a number of local practices including ancestor cult! Here are the very few words of Cardinal Man in a response to a question about his people giving up the cult of their ancestor: "We encourage the cult! After Vatican Council II, the Bishops of Vietnam used a pastoral letter telling Catholics to continue the practice. After all, God is the greatest ancestor. Then the question is: how can Africans develop when the continent is the home of violence and religious quagmire? Can't one be justified to say that Africa would remain poor as soon as it keeps embracing the strange religion at the detriment of the indigenous one that is married to the cultural environment of the continent?[88]

From the foregoing, and considering what obtains today, the Vietnamese Catholic Church is among the strongest of its kind today. That success was achieved because whilst establishing Catholicism in Vietnam, the church accorded indigenous culture its place. This differed from the approach in African communities. A recent instance of contempt for native customs was the banning of the inhumation ceremony in the Nsukka Diocese of Nigeria, on the ground that it intimated ancestor-worship.

Let me tell you what the Pink person means whenever they say 'Pink Jesus.' They simply mean that God is Pink and therefore Pink is good.

To palliate our alleged spiritual pains, Pink people sent forth our fellow Africans, clad in Pink cloaks, and dubbed them "Black preachers." They zealously discharged their duties, further enslaving their already enslaved kin, a situation which

---

88 Ibid, 56.

has resulted in the disintegration of our African community. What do we hear today? "Pray and forgive your enemy, and do not fight back." While these people killed us and continued our slavery, we prayed. I often ponder the prayers of us the slaves and those of our slave-masters. Perhaps we pray to be freed from our shackles, while our masters pray that our bondage might never end! The Lord is good!

Dearest sibling, do you not see that we have been stripped of our beliefs? We have been made to think like Pink people, our "praying and forgiving" masters. Our slavery is not even physical. No chains bind our hands; no padlocks keep us from flight. Our slavery survives in our minds and thrives in our instincts. Our ancestors who were enslaved first, bequeathed that bondsman mentality to their offspring, and it's been passed to us the descendants.

As has been stressed repeatedly, religion does us more harm than good. It is the chief cause of rifts in homes. False prophets have done much to cause discord in families; they tell childless young women that their mothers-in-law, by metaphysical devices, made them barren. Those credulous women would of course whirl into fierce and lengthy frays with their mothers-in-law. Wives and husbands neglect their family responsibilities to attend some church programme: *21 Days Power Packed Crusade, 40 Days and 40 Nights*. Their children might be dying of hunger and deprivation of parental nurture, whilst their parents focus unconcernedly on heaven.

Our slavery is furthered when Pink people tell and convince us that Jesus Christ is a Pink man. They suggest thereby that they, of the race and family of Jesus, are like gods and goddesses. We are tacitly made to accept that they the Pink people too must be worshipped.

In the face of all these, why will Africans not remain amateur till they wake to discover themselves?

SEVEN

ON MUSIC

I guess you may have thought that we would not get to this stage. You may be startled to read of music as a weapon in our enslavement. It is a bitter pill that I now share. I do not wish to know how much you like Western music, how much you prefer it to our indigenous music.

I shall be forthright and inform you that no detailed survey of the bastardization of our world would be complete without remarks on music. Music, like language, occupies a broad place in a people's culture, as philosophy, history and religion are often expressed in music. This could have informed Onwuegbuna's stance:

> *The omnipresence of music in the human society and its utilitarian stance in human life make the study of its cultural and philosophical essence a necessity. Though the functionality of music can be ascertained from a myriad of perspectives, it is often in the textual content*

> *and performance practices of folk songs that the ways of*
> *life and the general worldview of a people are exposed.*[89]

African societies in general, and the Igbo in particular, reflect this. A stranger uninformed about the Igbo outlook would gain considerable insights into it merely by listening to the renditions of some Igbo traditional musician.[90]

An instance of a homegrown item was written and explained by Onwuegbuna:

> *Opi m fugbuelumOmekagu; opi m fugbuelumOmekagu*
> *My horn, please, blow Omekagu to death*
> *Omekagulil' ji Mmuo; Omekagulil' ede Mmuo*
> *Omekagu ate the yam of the spirit, Omekagu ate the cocoyam of*
> *the spirit*
> *O bun'ifugbuelum Omekagu, fugbuelum Omekagu*
> *If you could just blow Omekagu to death, blow Omekagu to death*
> *Ka m wel'ebunugwayi aka*
> *So I could sacrifice a ram in appreciation.*
> *O bu n'ifugbuelum Omekagu, fugbuelum Omekagu*
> *If you could just blow Omekagu to death, blow Omekagu to death*
> *Ka m wel' ebunu gwayi aka*
> *So I could sacrifice a ram in appreciation*
> *Ma gi jide ogu, jide ofo; ma gi jideogu, jideofo*
> *But ensure you are just and fair; but ensure you are truly just*
> *and fair.*
> *Oh ghoo, oh gho-oghoo; oh ghoo, oh gho-oghoo!*[91]

---

89   Ikenna Emmanuel Onwuegbuna, *Music as an Embodiment of Culture and Philosophy: A Survey of Nigerian Folk Songs,* C. KrydzIkwuemesi (ed.), Astride Memory and Desire: Peoples, Culture and Development in Nigerian (Enugu:ABIC Books, 2012), 291.

90   A musical experience, expression, or composition that involves the setting of text to melody for vocal performance. Songs are metrically composed in verses.

91   Ibid, 296.

To portray the cultural message carried by the song, Onwegbuna writes thus:

> *The king, upon envisaging his imminent death from old age, assembled the elders and council of chiefs of his kingdom to introduce to them the heir apparent to the throne. But instead of presenting his first son, as the custom stipulates, the king presented his younger son, named Omekagu. His reason was that he loved Omekagu better, whom he had often praised beyond the skies; thereby spoiling him. This unjust deprivation of the right of progeniture of the first son was unacceptable to the elders and chiefs, who walked out on their king in disapproval. The king adamantly paraded Omekagu to his community on the appointed market day. It was as this parade progress that his aggrieved first son picked up the magical horn he received from the forest, and sounded the song. The result: the horn did as was implored, striking Omekagu to death; the King and the entire community apologized to the first son; he reversed the song of his magical horn; Omekagu resurrected; rightful heir was reinstated; and peace and harmony restored in the community.[92]*

Apart from Onwegbuna's explanation above, the story gives insights into Igbo philosophy. It is proof of the recognition of the possibility of wrong decisions; it suggests that people can and should stand even against a ruler where truth and principle demand that; it reflects faith in divine justice.

Chiefs and elders defied the King by leaving his palace

---

92 Ibid, 297.

when he presented the wrong person as successor to the throne. They were heedless of whatever royal punishment they might suffer. Furthermore, the first son who was unjustly deprived of his right, appealed to the gods to fight his cause. They acceded to his plea, and he emerged triumphant.

Furthermore, the song has revealed the god of the Igbo as merciful. His anger is short-lived; he is quick to forgive. Indeed, as portrayed, clemency is not peculiar to gods. Human Igbos are swift to pardon their offenders. The first son could not unperturbedly watch his brother end in untimely death. He not only forgave, but pleaded with the gods to restore his brother's life. That prayer was graciously answered. The King's character is reflected in another theme of the song. When the King realized his offence and its consequence, he was remorseful. Consequently, he humbled himself and begged forgiveness.

Many elements of the Igbo culture were alluded to in the above-quoted music. It reflects the past status quo in Igboland in particular, and Africa in general. Lamentably, this cultural heritage has been lost by the present-day African music industry, a loss caused by embrace of Western musical typology in the delusion that "West is right." When one listens to much of contemporary African music, one is puzzled about its concepts. The pieces seem to consist mainly of hollow lyrics. There is hardly a song with impressive cultural content. It is an appalling situation. We have no justification for allowing the Pink man's so-called colonization and civilization to efface our musical culture. As long as we persist in indiscriminate aping of the Pink people's singing and playing of instruments, we remain their slaves. We have casually jettisoned our rich musical culture, ensuring it could never again be found.

The juxtaposition of African indigenous music and the

Western-oriented ones prompted a book from me in January 2015. A book of music focused on the hip-hop music culture, which I titled *Hip Hop is Only for Children*. In crafting the book, I naturally expressed my personal perspectives on hip-hop culture. In the odyssey of hip-hop, I identified a Golden Age, as well as its Silver, Bronze and Stone ages. I dwelt in depth on the new generation of hip-hop, giving my critical appraisal of its Nigerian genre which is influenced by America. I discerned the differences, and again realized and bemoaned how much we had lost through clinging to Western trends.

I undertook that exercise because, being an ardent lover of music, I am aware of its importance in the cultures of the diverse societies and countries I have visited. I realize the essentiality of music in representing the heritage and cultural life of a people. Everything man does is grounded in music – dancing, story-telling and even religion – are based on music.

Reflecting on the importance of music, I note that we do not speak about it without reference to dance. In the past, before colonialism tore us apart, our people performed our music in our own way without copying from Pink people. We used it in child-naming ceremonies, initiation rites, agricultural activities, war, religions and funeral ceremonies.

During the slave trade, the Africans taken to North and South America and the Caribbean brought their music. Many African styles from various ethnic groups were forcefully merged with European dancing styles. Many African slaves strove to perform in indigenous mode in order to maintain their link to the homelands from which they had been torn. However, most slave owners in North America forbade their slaves to perform their traditional dances. The African slaves consequently performed their music in secret, and those who lacked the nerve to do so avoided music until it died in them.

However, some resourceful slaves devised a compromise. As they were forbidden to raise their feet in dance, they shuffled, moved their hips, and swayed their torsos.

Those African slaves also used musical instruments: drums, slit gongs, rattles, musical bows, forms of harps, flutes, stringed and wind instruments. They performed songs which had traditionally mobilized the masses, including the Zanla Forces war song of the people of Zimbabwe. They were songs of struggle used to spread the message of revolution. Some of those songs, like the Zanla war song, were sung purely vocally (acapella), as instruments were scarce. Much of African music is exceptional, calming or stirring, and worth sharing and preserving.

Although music entertained us in Africa, it was also, for us all, a way of life and a manifestation of cultural identity. Music is so important to us that some ceremonies cannot begin without a musical introduction to communicate, tell our stories, and welcome heroes into our rituals.

Africans love music, and therefore sing naturally. It serves as a medium of communication among men and women, and even between humans and spirits. Music is often used to ward off evil spirits, and pay homage to good ones and to the ancestors. From one African nation to another, there are variations in musical renditions, yet certain forms of musical expression are common to all. Although lots of instruments are employed, the African drum appears the most important because it expresses the mood of the people and even evokes emotion. It is often said that the beat of the African drum is the heart of the community, and what holds dancers together is the rhythm.

Dancing is very important in African music. It is an integral part of our culture. Oftentimes dancers use costumes, masks, body painting and props for symbolism and heightened communication. The movements of the body might be simple or complex, but most dances involve fast or slow rotation, ripples of the body, contraction and release. All those are highly symbolic and express joy or sorrow.

Nowadays, as I look around, I discover that those arts and skills have vanished from African societies, supplanted by the trend called 'hip-hop.' This is slavery!

It was American influence that brought hip-hop to Africa in the 1980s. It first got to Senegal, a Francophone country, in 1985. MC Lida, MC Solaar and Positive African Soul were the first Senegalese rappers, and they were the ones who mixed *Mbalax*, a West African Pop. They were followed by a South African group called "Black Noise," which began a graffiti and break-dance crew in Cape Town. Eventually, rap started spreading all over Africa.

What we call hip-hop today started in the streets of New York. It can be traced to a 13-year-old Jamaican émigré, Clive Campbell, who moved from Jamaica to New York, taking mobile discos and dub records of his birthplace. With those, he laid a strong foundation for the hip-hop movement.

Today, hip-hop music commands wide acclaim in many African nations. In Algeria, it is widely performed both by native Algerians and those of them living abroad. Many Algerians, although unknown internationally, have become popular hip-hop stars. There is hip-hop too in Angola, influenced by the hip-hop beats of Americans and the Caribbean.

In Nigeria where I come from, hip-hop started in Lagos in the late 80s and the early 90s. Nigeria was still under military rule, suffering a serious loss of jobs as well as the devaluation of its currency, the naira. Consequently, Nigerians youths resorted to hip-hop to save themselves from depression.

There were very few record labels, and those young people started funding themselves for their albums, with poor video production quality. In time, they upgraded their technology, using computers and editing software, duly producing videos which delighted audiences. Their songs were rendered mostly in English. Today in Nigeria, there are hip-hop magazines, television channels and radio stations all trumpeting that imported musical form, while native African music dies off.

The number of record labels in Botswana has increased greatly. The country is becoming mainstreamed. Several albums have been released, and there are numerous artists in the industry. A small market started the growth of the music industry in Botswana, but it has lately become prominent. Cameroon has also attained hip-hop limelight, with its pioneer hip-hop stars like Manhitoo and Negrissim, famous for breaking new grounds in the genre. Today, they have *Staney Enow* and *Jovi*, who have continued to trend.

The Ghanaian music scene has also produced a number of rappers and DJs, renowned both locally and internationally. Ghanaian rapping is mostly in the English language; hip-hop in Ghana is commonly referred to as *GH Rap*. The term *"GH Rap"* was created by the group "Jayson and Ball J" when they released their first Skillions mixtape. According to the two rappers, GH Rap means *hip-hop made in Ghana*. Hip-life, a Ghanaian genre similar to hip-hop music, is a blend of hip-hop music and highlife. It started in the late 1980s and early 90s, with the hip-life father, Reggie Rockstone, followed by VIP, Talking Drums, and Nananom.

In Madagascar, the local name of hip-hop is *"HaintsoHaintso"* meaning "H. H." (For Hip Hop). Malagasy hip-hop, although largely reflective of Western genre standards, has been moving towards more incorporation of the Malagasy musical tradition in style and instrumentation.

Hip-hop spread to Madagascar in about 1985, along with break-dancing. The local rap scene (Rap Gasy) remained underground until the late nineties, although as early as 1994, artists were attracting attention with their politically provocative lyrics. The earliest performers included the MCM Boys (now known as Da Hopp), and 18,3. Mainstream success came in about 1998. Popular modern performers include The Specialists, Paradisa, and Oratan.

In Uganda, hip-hop began in the early to mid-1990s, especially among university students at Makerere University and elsewhere. The Bataka Squad, formed in the early 1990s, are the originators of the Lugaflow style, using the native Luganda language. Other formative groups on the Ugandan hip-hop scene in the early 90s include Young Vibrations, MC Afrik, DJ Berry, Sylvester and Abramz and Kaddo. Club Pulsations in Kampala was a hotspot for Ugandan hip-hop in the 90s. In recent years, groups such as KlearKut, Milestone, Chain Thought Reaction and many more have emerged. In 2002, KlearKut were nominated for the Kora All Africa Music Awards in the "Most Promising African Group" and "Revelation of the Year" categories.

These are examples of how new music trends, from Europe and America, have captured the entire music scene in Africa. Of course the masters' incursion was unobstructed, because we the slaves loved whatever they did.

Dear sibling, in all the musical feats by African people enumerated above, where lies our heritage? Where is our indigenous African music? Where is our Benga of the Luo people of Kenya? Where is our Apala, of the Yoruba people of Nigeria? Where is the Jive of the South Africans? Where is our own Jali, for our storytellers? Where is the famous Juju, the one for which Sunny Ade was known? Where is our own Afrobeat, the form of Africa's music god, Fela Anikulapo-Kuti? Where are they? We have buried them because we are ashamed of them, because we are proud only of whatever comes from Pink people. Who says this is not slavery?

EIGHT

ON POLITICS

I believe you have an idea of what "politics" means because it is an everyday term. You as well may have engaged in it one way or another. Before we proceed to examine how politics has affected us since our contact with the Pink man, I want to briefly define the term. In doing so, however, I will reproduce what Anyanw;'l; says about politics:

> *Politics has no widely accepted definition. Different scholars have varying definitions of the concept. Osagheas quoted in Madukwe (2005) defined it as that which has to do with power relations (and how) individuals or groups organize to pursue their divergent and often conflicting interest[93] Elucidating this, Madukwe noted that politics as "**that introduced by the colonizers was used to pursue the divergent and often conflicting policies of the British rule in***

93 [1]Madukwe, Chinyere Isaac, (2005), as quoted in Anyanwu Timothy, A Study of the Ethno-Religious Conflicts in Nigeria's Political System, 1960-1999, An unpublished MSc Project. Peace Studies and Conflict Resolution Department, National Open University of Nigeria, July, 2017.

> **her Nigerian colony**[94].[95] *This is to say that politics is
> a means to determining the percentage of the national
> resources that one gets. According to the American
> political scientist, Harold Lasswell as quoted in Jonas
> (2007), Politics is defined as that act that determines
> "who gets what, when and how."*[96] *Jonas emphasized
> that politics involves allocation of society's scarce
> resources among individuals, groups, regions, and social
> classes. It also deals with the production and allocation
> of resources.*[97] *The forgoing explains why politics in
> Nigeria is a do or die affair. It is a process that leads to
> the crest of national power acquisition. And once one
> gets there, he can have as much chunk as he wants from
> the "national cake".*[98]

From the above description, it is imperative to assert that, apart from enslaving the African people and helping their declining British economy, the British started imperialism in order to force their system of government upon us – their slaves. As you already know, the system of government which Pink people imposed on us has never done us any good. Arriving with devious plans, they overpowered us, and assumed control of our destiny. This, it must be repeated, was accomplished by force. They were at the helm in virtually all that concerned the African man. In this chapter, I aim to look into the politics which Pink people imposed on us, how we

94 Emphases are mine
95 10³Madukwe, Chinyere Isaac, (2005), as quoted in Anyanwu Timothy.
96 10⁴Austin Shively, as quoted in Anyanwu Timothy.
97 10⁵Jonas OlisaemekaEze, as quoted in Anyanwu Timothy.
98 Anyanwu Timothy, A Study of the Ethno-Religious Conflicts in Nigeria's Political System, 1960-1999, An unpublished M.Sc. Project. Peace Studies and Conflict Resolution Department, National Open University of Nigeria, July, 2017.

assimilated it as slaves without a choice, and the consequences of that acceptance.

We all know that the British is full of greed. Here is the issue: When the British realized that their economy was declining as a result of the American Revolution, they sought means to stabilize it. The result was that the British, known for trade, started looking for countries to sell their wares. When they could not succeed, they chose imperialism, a policy of forceful extension of a nation's authority over others, to nurture the overreaching nation. Being proud of their nation, the British were determined to improve their economy, and therefore established more territories.

They overpowered Africa within a few years, seizing her palm oil in other to lubricate industrial plants in Britain. It happened that when the Suez Canal was opened in Egypt, it provided the British with a shorter route to India, which became the brightest jewel of British imperialism. The grasping British craved more land in Africa to consolidate its might and protect its other territories from acquisition by other nations. They were convinced that other countries wanted to assume control of India. To prevent other nations' easy access to India, the British bought control of the Suez Canal. By 1882, Britain controlled all of Egypt. Still convinced that other countries would hold sway over India, the British also took over South Africa. Of course before the Suez Canal was opened, ships from Europe almost circled Africa to reach India, sailing past South Africa. South Africa was the perfect stop for refueling. In 1870 when gold and diamonds were discovered in South Africa, it became even more attractive to British Imperialists. After the British gained control of South Africa and Egypt, they continued to acquire other lands. Thanks to wars in other countries, the British never faced much competition over its acquisition of territories. Their own wars over, the French and the Germans also started to crave land in Africa. Land was cheap in Africa, and Africans lacked the weapons to crush European incursion. The British, determined to best other western powers in Africa, secured as much land as they could. They wanted theirs to be the richest and most powerful empire in the world.

When British rule was consolidated in Africa, they established the indirect rule colonial administration. It featured harsh and intimidating laws. Territories were governed by local rulers, and the British encouraged the children of those rulers to acquire formal education. Thus, in the British colonies, power was retained in certain exclusive circles. Those offspring of local potentates ended up with imperialist convictions. They assumed they must rule their people who lacked their education. They thought nothing of using Pink people's armies and police to subdue or penalize rebellious factions in their own African race.

My fellow Africans, the power of the British duly declined in some countries, including Egypt. Egypt gained its independence. However, British influence pervaded the entire African race. We embraced their ways, espousing Christianity and Islam. Despite our claims to independence, we still cling to the Pink outlook and mode of life.

Now, let us use South Africa as a case study. Sometime ago, a war broke out among the Boers, the Zulus and Britain. At some stage, about 5,000 migrants were persuaded to settle on the land between the groups as buffers. About half of those settlers had emigrated into South Africa, and they secured jobs similar to the ones they had had in Britain. South Africans naturally became indignant, and were moved to further fury by being frustrated by Pink men. Pink men pranced about like demigods, and even declared that their supremacy was divinely decreed. They promulgated new laws which made them South Africa's masters, while the natives became slaves. A faction of the Boers broke away, and were called the *Voortrekkers*. Migrating to another location in search of fertile land, they became embroiled in a fierce battle with the Zulus, who would neither yield nor compromise over ownership of their own land. Although the *Voortrekkers* lost the battle, many Zulus were slaughtered. Boer resentment of the British deepened when in 1843, the land that Boers had fought near Natal, was annexed by the British. In 1877, the Boers defeated the British at the battle of Majuba, gaining their independence as the South African Republic. As the Pink Boers outnumbered the British, British reaction took the form of a plan to unite all of South Africa under British rule, impacting it with British culture, making the English language (and later Dutch) its official languages.

The Pink man organized his colonies at the central, provincial, regional and district levels. There were governors or governors-general in the colonial capital who governed with an appointed Executive Council, and a Legislative Council of appointed and selected local and foreign members. The governors were responsible to the Colonial Office and the Colonial Secretary in London, from whom they received laws, policies, and programs.

My Dearest Sibling, the French Colonialists had the conviction that they were on a 'civilizing mission.' The French used the policy of assimilation on African Natives. By this policy, they claimed that by acculturation, education and the fulfillment of certain conditions, some natives would become fully evolved and socialized French Africans. They established a highly centralized administrative system that was influenced by colonialist ideology. However, they enforced stringent laws that prevented colonial subjects from assuming full French citizenship. The French expected a potential citizen to speak fluent French, serve the French Empire impressively, win an award for active service or prove in some other respect exceptional. One reflects that only a minuscule percentage of colonial subjects could fulfill those criteria. Of course that system created the gratifying situation where the African people remained in thrall of the Pink.

In his essay *"The Colonization of Africa",* published in *The Exhibition,* Iweriebor Ehiedu opines that "The French man used the direct rule method in their various colonies in Algeria, Tunisia, and even Morocco in North Africa; Senegal, French Guinea, French Sudan, Upper Volta, Dahomey, and others in West Africa; and Gabon, Congo-Brazzaville, Ubangi-Shari in Central Africa. They were responsible to the Minister of the Colonies in Paris, and they established federations in West and Central Africa. The colonies were also subdivided into smaller administrative units as follows: Cercles, under Commandant du Cercles, subdivisions under chef de subdivisions, and at the next level, cantons, which were administered by African chiefs, who were in effect like the British warrant chiefs."

Whoever advised the French to adopt the system of association must be very smart. With this system, they operated with an alliance with the pre-existing African rulers, whilst maintaining their assimilation. The local governments were run by African rulers whom the French organized at three basic levels: Chef de Province (provincial chief); Chef de Canton (district chiefs), and Chef de Village (village chief).

Although the French combined the systems of indirect and direct rule, their administration was more centralized, bureaucratic, and interventionist than Britain's colonial rule. The other colonial powers – Germany, Portugal, Spain, Belgium, and Italy – used varied administrative systems to facilitate suppression and economic exploitation of Africans. The essential objective was – and remains – the perpetuation of African enslavement.

NINE

ON TRIBALISM

I f we lie to every other person or persons, we should never lie to ourselves. If we have been lying to ourselves, we should not persist in deceit. It is time to tell ourselves the truth, however bitter it might be. We have been stripped of virtually everything, including the unity and love which used to be our hallmarks. In this chapter, let us examine how Pink men turned blood relations against one another in the name of civilization.

Tribalism is the greatest harm the coming of the Pink man inflicted on us African people. They accomplished this by depriving us of the duty and dignity of building our own nations on our own indigenous values, institutions, and heritage. They defined our lives, even giving us names which we continue to bear today. Hence, they defined our destinies, and placed us wherever they assumed suitable. I therefore ask you all: is there any form of slavery greater than this? I am yet to see any punishment greater than denying someone their ethnicity. I believe that anyone who is being denied their ethnicity has equally been denied their identity, their sense of purpose and direction.

We functioned through our family lineage, our clans, the tribes, and a confederation of groups with their ethnic, cultural and linguistic attributes. Those were the units of our social, economic and political organizations.

Pink people welded groups together for colonial state formation, with no thought of common characteristics or attributes. The peoples were placed in a new administrative structure, governed by new rules, new principles and methods. The control mechanism of the new states was established, in which of course authority was the ultimate preserve of the Pink people. This evil mechanism was upheld by the might of the police, the military, and other instruments of authoritarian rule.

Our Pink masters never bothered to consider our cultural attributes before their numerous mergers of diverse groups. This attitude was borne of the fact that they considered us inconsequential; they thought we were subhuman quantities who would accept whatever structures were forced upon them. Still, in that slavish mentality, the founding fathers of the Organization of African Unity maintained the borders established by the colonial masters. The OAU fought against secessionist movements. Katanga's failed struggle to break away from the Congo, Biafra's bid to be independent of Nigeria, and Southern Sudan's thwarted seventeen-year-old effort to leave the North, are instances.

What has tribalism brought us? It creates assumptions of superiority and inferiority among tribes. Members of one tribe despise those of another and exact servitude and subservience from the disdained group. Tribalists deploy those attitudes to further their ignoble interests. They now boast of attributes which make them special and place them above other tribes. Their conceit and brusqueness mar African nationhood.

It was tribalism that created liberalism and favoritism in African communities. A tribe, assuming itself to be special, confers privileges and high posts on its indigenes, exempting them from tasks considered humble or demeaning. Tribal favoritism is rampant in the apportionment of privileges and benefits in African nations. It exists in marriage, when a member of a certain tribe feels that someone from another is unworthy, on the ground of ethnic origin, to be their marriage partner. I repeat that tribalism prevails in public life, influencing the distribution of administrative and political power.

My fellow Africans, tribalism is hideous in all its ramifications. I wish to relate an incident in Kenya a few years ago. As observers of East African politics know that Daniel Arap Moi had seized power. What was his mission? It was to be revenged on the Kalenjin ethnic group for their alleged suppression of the Kikuyu. In Ethiopia, a similar situation unfolded. The regime of the Ethiopian Revolutionary Democratic Front (EPRDF) held sway for ten years of draconian rule, mainly intent on achieving Tigrayans' domination of the allegedly predominant Amhara ruling class.

Of the Igbo tribe from which I sprang, there have been violent clashes – with fatalities – between Igbo and non-Igbo groups in Northern Nigeria, and in Owerri and Port-Harcourt in the South. Similar crises have erupted between the Yoruba and the Hausa in Ibadan.

Festering resentment caused such incidents in 1960s Uganda. Behind it were accusations against members of ethnic groups who were supportive of the Baganda. That bitterness bred calamity.

In many cases, the enmity has endured for decades. The stories – and the fury – are handed down through generations.

Tribalism affects every sphere of development, from the social, economic to political to educational. It is now a channel for sharing the bounties of the state. Most people tend to be loyal to their tribes, rather to the nation. Ethnic loyalty definitely precedes nationhood. In Nigeria, it was given the euphemistic, sanitizing name of "national character!" In employment today, jobs are given to applicants of the "right" ethnic group, however deficient their qualifications or general fitness for the posts. The effect of this trend on national development is grave. It is definitely a massive scourge on African nations.

The underdevelopment which today characterizes many African countries is caused by tribalism. The corruption, the rigging of elections, violence and battles, are all consequences of tribalism. Bad government and lack of accountability are also other yield of tribalism. The tribal influence in politics has created poor service delivery alike in public and private spheres.

Of all African nations, Ethiopia stands out in at least one respect. After the breakaway of Eritrea, Ethiopia confronted the challenge of tribalism by recognizing ethnic groups on territorial bases, granting them autonomy with the constitutional rights of self-determination and secession. The truth is that when people's rights to determine their destinies are recognized, they are assured that their interests matter.

We cannot deny the fact that the modern African state is the handiwork of European conquest. The massive work of restructuring, re-conceptualizing, and reconstituting the state, requires the cooperation of Africa's global partners. Where are those partners? What have they done to divest themselves of the chains of slavery? Nothing!

A few years ago, I had a long discussion on this issue with

someone. He opined that we could achieve the desired goal only with the help of external forces. Who are these outside forces? Obviously Pink men, the people that caused our present rut.

My dear Sibling, we must commence an arduous mission of rediscovery and restoration of indigenous values. Until we do this, we will still be slaves.

TEN

ON MIGRATION

I wish you would find time to visit the US Embassies in any African country. You would agree with me that the numbers of African people trying to immigrate to the US and Europe increase daily. In this chapter, I wish to expatiate on how we Africans are slaves and will remain slaves as long as we continue on the path of migration.

In 2013, there were 1.8 million African migrants living in the US. African migrants formed a large percentage of the people in the US. Records and research show that this figure is rises every year. In previous chapters, I wrote extensively about how a lot of Africans were brought to the U.S as slaves, to work on the farms and in the courtyards of masters who treated them like puppets. Now that we are long past the era of the Trans-Atlantic Slave Trade, we are in the epoch when migration has made us slaves.

Each new day brings news of Africans who died whilst trying to cross the Sahara Desert, or drowned in the Mediterranean. They embarked on those hazardous journeys because they were weary of their lives in Africa. Of course, some succeed in arriving their lands of promise, while many, overcome by harsh Sahara weather, end up as dinner to vultures. Nigeria, Ethiopia, Ghana, Egypt and Kenya have been noted as having the highest number of African migrants in the US.

On November 1, 2013, the *Daily Mail* reported the deaths of 92 men and women from the Niger who were trying to cross the Sahara Desert to migrate. Their lifeless bodies were found strewn in the desert. Graves were dug and they were buried.

Most migrants now enter Libya from where they begin their journey to Europe. They pay heavily to board rickety old boats for their trip. Many are captured in transit, while many others die during the voyage. The yearning for Europe continually swells among Africans. When the Italian government realized how Africans were surging illegally to Europe, they launched what we know today as *Operation Mare Nostrum*.

Bids to reduce the number of Africans migrating to Europe and America have not solved the problem of migration. The population of the developing countries daily increase, just as the urge to migrate continually spread and intensifies.

My fellow Africans, those Pink nations are pleased to see Africans scurrying and scrambling to enter Europe and America. They cannot but feel superior to see people risking their lives, sometimes paying the ultimate prize, to come to their nations. Now, they have realized that the maligned migration is important for their economic growth. According to the explanation given by the World Bank, if the labour force in high-income countries were to grow by 3%, there would be $356 billion in annual global gains. This indicates the advantages of African migration to industrialized nations.

Some of those countries are now searching for migrants.

They wish to enhance their economies and lifespan. There is need for more workers in the information sector, health, agriculture, and even construction.

While we discuss those countries' need for labour, it must be remembered that they can only accept and absorb limited numbers of migrants periodically. Even many of the nations of the European Union have been experiencing severe unemployment. Consequently, they are very selective over the quality of migrants they could accept in their countries.

How do we solve the problem of African people's mania for migrating to Europe and America? We can start by asking what attracts them to those countries. Obviously, they yearn to flee the difficulties of life at home: unemployment, poverty and strife. There are few job opportunities in most African countries; few rewards for ability and industry. The governments have not done much to reverse that sad situation. In a country like Nigeria, many who work are owed their salaries for months or years. To remain in those jobs eventually appears idiotic. Those who worked and retired are owed their pensions. They spend years going to offices, repeatedly assembling and processing documents in order to receive their pensions. Some have collapsed and died in the offices where they went to process their pensions. People from war-ravaged zones in Africa also long for the supposed peace and order of foreign climes.

Why can't the African build their land to suit their taste? Why can't we fight to install in our lands, the comforts we seek in Europe and America?

ELEVEN

ON TERRORISM

Africa is a very porous land, where any monkey can easily jump in and leave without being questioned. The result is that we experience a lot of conflicts, both internal and external. This chapter seeks to analyze those conflicts, and Africans' failure to resolve them because we wait on the assistance of our masters. It also examines how Islamic extremists afflicted Africa with the terror which continues to sweep across the continent.

Due to our borders' penetrability, we have incursions by unwanted guests who mar African lives. As is usually the case, leaders entrusted with the security of citizens' lives and property are lax in the discharge of their duties. They are either incapable of rising to the challenge of their charge, or simply nonchalant over that charge. Their attitude makes citizens vulnerable; in many cases, it results in loss of lives. Those lofty but negligent officials are guarded and escorted by armies, perhaps even when they go to the lavatory. As they are insulated from the security issues which blight other lives, they serenely enjoy their pampered lives. Furthermore, as those leaders keep their children in the Western world, they are understandably unconcerned about our nations' security.

Even as I write, terrorist activities explode in various parts of Africa. In my country Nigeria, there is insurgency in the North. This is being perpetrated by the notorious Islamic sect, Boko Haram. Its adherents have achieved the feat of murdering thousands in bomb blasts, and destroyed properties worth billions of naira. They spawned a splinter group which kidnaps civilians in Northern Nigeria.

Kaduna, Borno, Kano, and Adamawa are only four of the states in Nigeria where those terrorists have executed their attacks. When security operatives are being killed, what becomes the fate of unprotected civilians? Even diplomats have been kidnapped. Some were freed after they had paid huge ransoms; others had the trigger pulled on them.

When we slaves discovered that we could actually accomplish nothing without our masters, we requested the masters' aid. This led to the formation of the Nigeria-US Counterterrorism Cooperation. Years later, the Nigerian Government formally requested a Joint Terrorism Branch (JTAB) to aid the sharing of information. Despite the many calls for aid from the slaves to the masters, terrorism rages on.

In June 2014, Abubakar Usaman, in his essay *"2014: A Timeline of Boko Haram Attacks in Nigeria,"* provided a comprehensive list of the terrorist attacks of the dreaded sect:

> ***February 15, 2014****: An attack blamed on the extremist sect leaves more than 100 people dead in the mostly Christian village of Izghe in the North-Eastern State of Borno.*
>
> ***April 14****: Gunmen kidnap 276 female high school students in Chibok, Borno. Fifty-seven managed to escape but the rest are still being held. Several foreign countries, including the United States, have joined forces to try to find the girls.*

April 14: *A blast at a bus station packed with morning commuters at Nyanya, on the southern outskirts of Abuja, kills at least 75 people, the most deadly attack to date on the capital. Boko Haram claims responsibility. On May 1, a car bomb at the same spot kills 19, and leaves 80 injured.*

May 5: *At least 300 people are killed in an attack in Gamboru Ngala, in Borno State near the border with Cameroon, which totally destroys the town.*

May 20: *At least 118 are killed and 56 injured in two car bomb attacks on a market in Jos, central Nigeria, which go off within 20 minutes of each other. The regional governor blames Boko Haram.*

June 1: *At least 40 are killed when a bomb explodes at a football stadium in Mubi in the North-East of the country shortly after a match. The attack is blamed on Boko Haram.*

June 3: *Hundreds are feared dead in a suspected Boko Haram attack on four villages in Borno State, with local leaders putting the death toll as high as 500.*

June 17: *21 football fans are killed when a bomb rips through the viewing centre where they are watching the World Cup in Damaturu, Northern Nigeria.*

June 24: *Local officials report 30 killed and more than 60 women kidnapped in a series of attacks over several days in Borno State, although the Nigerian government denies the abductions.*

June 25: *At least 21 people are killed and 17 injured in a bombing at a crowded shopping centre in the centre of Abuja. The attack – the third on the city in three months – is blamed on Boko Haram.*

June 29: *Suspected Boko Haram gunmen riding on motorcycles target a number of churches during Sunday mass, opening fire on worshippers and chasing them into the bush. Witnesses fear dozens are killed."*

All these were just done in one year. Huffington Post declared Boko Haram the world's deadliest group, after it was recorded that the group killed 6,664 people in 2014 alone. Of course their bloodletting did not stop, continuing in 2015. All those slaughters persist in Nigeria because of utter lack of coordination among Nigeria's security agencies, and endemic corruption.

In East Africa today, Somalia faces a similar problem perpetrated by the terrorist group, "Al-Shabaab." They have successfully carried out numerous terrorist attacks. According to the 2009 paper published in the Middle East Quarterly by Daveed Garstein-Ross, titled *"The Strategic Challenge of Somalia's Al-Shabaab;"* that military group, "rose from obscurity to international prominence in two years." The group has claimed responsibility for most terrorist attacks in Somalia, including the bombing of the Chinese Embassy and the killing of 147 students in a Kenyan University.

Burkina Faso is not left out in terrorist attack. Even though its Federal Government has adopted measures to fight Al-Qaeda, the battle is yet to be won. In such countries as Burundi, Cameroon, Chad, Kenya, and Mali, a like situation exists.

Sibling, all these terrorist groups have very strong roots in the Islamic religion which was brought down to us by the Pink man.

Osama bin Laden founded Al-Qaeda, and their major aim was to establish a Muslim State throughout the world. This group can be called the live-wire of other extremist groups in Nigeria, as it is responsible for funding the activities of the different extremist groups. What did they not do? They now have links to other bigger groups that have continued to threaten and kill African people.

Algerian leaders have not been freed from the shackles of the armed Islamist group, which refuses to relent in its homicidal mission. Today, its members are all over the land of Yemen. Harakat Ul-Mujahidinis is another Islamist terror group, as well as Jaish-e-Mohammed and Lashkar-i-Taiba.

Fellow African, we naturally rage against the terrorism which religion, an arm of colonization, inflicted on us. We should also rage against other unsaid ills which Africans brought upon themselves, and which continue to trap us in slavery. James J. F. Forest, in his essay *"Terrorism and Political Violence in Africa: Contemporary Trends in a Shifting Terrain,"* notes that Africa has its own forms of domestic violence. He notes some of them when he opines that "…there are also irresponsible governments that have employed the tactics of terrorism in (for example) a brutal crackdown against opposition leaders in Zimbabwe, or the Eritrean government's support (according to a recent UN report) for terrorist plots against African leaders gathering in Ethiopia. President Omar al-Bashir of Sudan is the first sitting head of state to be indicted by the International Criminal Court for crimes against humanity, while in the newly independent South Sudan, locals are calling for a war crimes investigation. In Senegal, riots erupted in the streets to protest President Abdoulaye Wade's attempt to change the constitution in an effort to be elected for another term in office. Add to that the tragic episodes of genocide in places like Rwanda and the Darfur region of Sudan and you have a first glimpse of the atrocities that the present African generation has witnessed."

LAST WORDS

It is no news that Africans played their part in enabling European greed and arrogance to plunder the continent. Under the guise of colonialism or evangelization, Africans were psychologically manipulated to reject themselves. They were made to accept inferiority. They were made to be comfortable with being mediocre. The consequent mindset keeps the continent in a dismal state, as it appears a barrier that could never be surmounted. It has kept many African countries from attaining peace. Conditions forced on us by our colonial masters thwarted all our efforts to develop our economies. Political instability and war for control of government are commonplace in Africans' daily lives. Innumerable Africans have been displaced. Properties too have been destroyed or lost, all because of colonialism.

Despite all the harrowing facts outlined, I would still conclude with the declaration that although "things have fallen apart" in Africa, the centre could still be put together. After all, at a stage in European history, there was a cultural hiatus, with alien values and modes invading and dominating nations. Those overcome Europeans were disorientated, just like today's Africans. Yet they took stock, and strove to restore what they had lost. Afigbo has important suggestions for African people:

> *The movement in European history generally known as Renaissance (meaning rebirth, reawakening, and revival) has often been described as having aimed at return to cultural achievements of ancient Greece and Rome. This is because it arose, to some extent, from the belief or conviction among Eastern Europeans of the Fifteenth and early Sixteenth centuries that the period of their history stretching from the fall of Roman Empire in the West (476AD) to the capture of Constantinople by the Turk (1453) constituted a kind of **cultural and intellectual hiatus in their history**[99], a period during which the great secular humanistic culture of European antiquity was smothered, first, by the barbarism of the Germanic tribes who destroyed the Roman Empire in the west and second, by Christianity with its otherworldly orientation which dwarfed man, his talent, his genius and his intrinsic worth. Through the Renaissance, the Western Europeans saw themselves as men involved in making a great leap from their own time across a huge and arid chasm which they called the Middle Ages to the world of ancient Greeks and Romans which they cherished greatly as a golden age.[100]*

His argument is that the Africans should return to their roots just as Europeans did when they realized how far they had strayed from their core philosophies. The cultures that nurtured the ancestors should be rediscovered and cherished as was done in Europe. Only by so doing would the bridges and barricades built by Europeans during colonialism be destroyed. Unless those shackles of our enslavement are broken, Africans remain in bondage.

---

99 Emphasis are mine
100 Afigbo, Towards Cultural Revival, 4.

ACKNOWLEDGEMENTS

I started working on this book years ago, in 2016, when I became a Visiting Research Fellow at Ohio University. Thanks to Dr. Negash Ghirmai for inviting me. I am thankful to Professor Amrijit Singh, for his kindness and fatherly love. I owe you.

I thank Nobel Laureate, Professor Wole Soyinka, for that dinner in Dakar, Senegal and for listening to me all the time. It was because of him that I had the privilege to sit with Professor Henry Louis Gates Jr.

Through the years I worked on this book, I was lucky to have all kinds of perspectives and input, to shape it. I thank: Hymar David, Cheta Igbokwe, Raphael Adebayo, MacDonald Ukah, Mitterand Okorie, Ebelenna Esomnofu, Timothy Anyanwu, Edaoto and others who refused to be mentioned.

I am grateful to Dr. David Pratten, who made it possible for me to join the African Studies Centre, University of Oxford. Grateful to Professor Miles Larmer.

Thanks to Emmanuel Ikechukwu Umeonyirioha, Ikenna Okeh, Kelvin Kellman, David Lanre Messan and members of the James Currey Society.

Thanks to my assistant, Ifeanyi Mojekwu and Anne Nwakalor and everyone at Abibiman Publishing, for the support.

I may not have written the names of the people who generously contributed to this project, financially. But, I am super grateful and indebted to them.

Thank you!

BIBLIOGRAPHY

Achebe, Chinua. *Things Fall Apart*. London: Heinemann Educational Books Ltd, 1958.

Afigbo, E.A. *Towards Cultural Revival Amongst the Igbo-Speaking Peoples,* (eds.)Ugo Agada and Kemjika Anoka: Anu Magazine, 3., 4.

African Year Book and Who's Who 1977, eds. Raph Uwechue et.al, London: Africa Journal Limited Kirkman House, 1076.

Ajayi, J.F.A. and J.B. Webster, *The Emergence of a New Elite in Africa,* Joseph C. Anene and Godfrey N. Brown eds. *Africa in the Nineteenth and Twentieth Centuries,* Ibadan: University Press, 1966.

Akubueze Oluchi Blessing (2011) *Ethno-Religious Crisis in Nigeria (A Case Study of Jos Crisis). An Unpublished BA Project, History and International Studies Department, Imo State University, Owerri.*

Anene, J. C. *The People of Benin, the Niger Delta, Congo and Angola in the Nineteenth Century,* Joseph C. Anene and Godfrey N. Brown eds. *Africa in the Nineteenth and Twentieth Centuries,* Ibadan: University Press, 1966.

Anyanwu Timothy Chibuike, A Study of the Ethno-Religious Conflicts in Nigeria's Political System, 1960-1999, An unpublished M.Sc. Project. Peace Studies and Conflict Resolution Department, National Open University of Nigeria, July, 2017.

Anyanwu Timothy Chibuike, The Social and Economic Impacts of the Iwa-Akwa Ceremony In Ehime Mbano, Imo State: 1960- 2013.Unpublished B.A. Project, Department of History and International Studies, University of Nigeria, Nsukka, July, 2015.

Asante Molefi Kete. *The History of Africa: The Question for Eternal Harmony*, New York: Routledge, 2007.

Ayandele, E.A. *External Influence on African Society,* Joseph C. Anene and Godfrey N. Brown eds. *Africa in the Nineteenth and Twentieth Centuries,* Ibadan: University Press, 1966.

Basden, G.T. *Niger Ibos: A Description of the Primitive Life, Custom, and Animistic Belief of the Ibo People of Nigeria By One Who, for Thirty Five Years Enjoyed the Privilege of Their Intimate Confidence and Friendship,* (London: Frank-Cass Pub. Company Limited, 1966.

Bodley, John H. "Culture." Microsoft® Student 2009 [DVD]. Redmond, WA: Microsoft Corporation, 2008.

Cell, John W. "Colonialism and Colonies."Microsoft® Encarta® 2009 [DVD]. Redmond, WA: Microsoft Corporation, 2008.

Chukwu, Kabiri Kenneth. *Transnational Corporations and African Nations,* African *Politics*: eds. Emezi C.E and Ndoh C.A., Owerri: Achugo Publications 1998.

Edwards, Paul. (eds.), *Equiano's Travels,* London, 1967.

Ejikeme, Joy. *Marketing Nigerian Cultural Heritage: A Boon to National Development* C. Krydz Ikwuemesi (ed.), Astride Memory and Desire: Peoples, Culture and Development in Nigerian, Enugu:ABIC Books, 2012.

Emezi, Cletus E. *Decolonization Process in Africa: A Critical*

Reflection, African *Politics*: eds. Emezi C.E and Ndoh C.A., Owerri: Achugo Publications 1998.

Ezeh, Peter-Jazzy. *Religion, Cultural Hegemony and Post-Colonial Social Order in Africa,* C. Krydz Ikwuemesi (ed.), Astride Memory and Desire: Peoples, Culture and Development in Nigerian, Enugu:ABIC Books, 2012.

Faleti, S.A, and Durojaye O.B, (2013) *Ethnic Conflict and Resolution,* Abuja: National Open University of Nigeria.

Ijoma, Okoro J. Igboland Till Present, A lecture Delivered to Final Year Students, History and International Studies Department, University of Nigeria, Nsukka, February 2015.

Kenneth, Obiekwe. *Place of Culture in Human Rights: A Theologico-Moral Study of Iwa-akwa* Owerri: Faycan Limited, 1998.

Korie, Chima, *Africa and the Wider World,* Lecture delivered to third year students of History and International Studies of University of Nigeria, Nsukka, February, 2015.

Legum, Colin. *Nationalism in South Africa,* Joseph C. Anene and Godfrey N. Brown eds. *Africa in the Nineteenth and Twentieth Centuries,* (Ibadan: University Press, 1966.

Madukwe, Isaac Chinyere. *Towards A Re-Evaluation of Moral Values in Nigeria,* C. Krydz Ikwuemesi (ed.), Astride Memory and Desire: Peoples, Culture and Development in Nigerian Enugu: ABIC Books, 2012.

Ndoh C.A. *Colonial System of Administration in Africa: A Comparative Review,* African *Politics*: eds. Emezi C.E and Ndoh C.A., Owerri: Achugo Publications 1998.

Nwankwo ,BasilChukwuemeka, *Colonialism and its Impact in Africa,* African *Politics*: eds. Emezi C.E and Ndoh C.A., Owerri: Achugo Publications 1998.

Nwosu, Petermary. *Transnational Corporations (TNCs) and Third*

World Security and Defence, African *Politics*: eds. Emezi C.E and Ndoh C.A., Owerri: Achugo Publications 1998.

Oddey, Michael. "Nigeria, 1900-1960", a Lecture delivered to the Third Year Students of History and International Department, University of Nigeria, Nsukka, on 02 December 2014.

Ofeimun, Odia. *Nigeria the Beautiful: Poems for Dance Drama,* Lagos: Hornbill House of the Arts, 2011.

Ofoebe, Chikelu. The Development Process in Africa: The Taxonomy of a Continental Phenomenon: African Politics, ed. Emezi, C.E and Ndoh, C.A. Owerri: Achugo Publications 1998.

Ogbajie, Chukwu.*The Impact of Christianity on the Igbo Religion and Culture, Umuahia: Ark Publishers, 1995.*

Ojiako, James O. *Nigeria: yesterday, Today and…?,*Onitsha: Africana Educational Publishers (Nig.) Ltd.

Omer-Cooper, J.D.*South Africa from the Great Trek to Unification,* Joseph C. Anene and Godfrey N. Brown eds. *Africa in the Nineteenth and Twentieth Centuries,* Ibadan: University Press, 1966.

Omer-Cooper J.D. *The Mfecane and the Great Trek.*Joseph C. Anene and Godfrey N. Brown eds. *Africa in the Nineteenth and Twentieth Centuries,* Ibadan: University Press, 1966.

Onwuegbuna, EmmanuelIkenna. *Music as an Embodiment of Culture and Philosophy: A Survey of Nigerian Folk Songs,* C. KrydzIkwuemesi (ed.), Astride Memory and Desire: Peoples, Culture and Development in Nigerian Enugu:ABIC Books, 2012.

OnwukaNjoku, *Economic History of Nigeria, 19th -21st Centuries* (second edition) Nsukka: Great AP Express Publishers Ltd, 2014.

Paul Abii-Ndoh and P.C. Ngoka, *The World Bank and the Third*

World, African *Politics*: eds. Emezi C.E and Ndoh C.A., Owerri: Achugo Publications 1998) 154.

Peterson, Wallace C. "Capitalism." Microsoft® Encarta® 2009 [DVD]. Redmond, WA: Microsoft Corporation, 2008.

Subrahmanyam, *Our National Security*" quoted in in Peter Nwosu, *Transnationa Corporations (TNCs) and Third World Security Defence,*African *Politics*: eds. Emezi C.E and Ndoh C.A., Owerri: Achugo Publications 1998.

Tabb, William K. "Globalization." Microsoft® Student 2009 [DVD]. Redmond, WA: Microsoft Corporation, 2008.

Talbot, P.A. *The People of Southern Nigeria Volume 3,* (London: Frank-Cass Publishing Company, 1937.

The Amended Burial as Per-Custom and Tradition of Umuomanwoke

Ugwu,Chidi. *Indigenous Stranger: The Social Psychology of the Perception and Application of Culture in Nigeria*, C. KrydzIkwuemesi (ed.), Astride Memory and Desire: Peoples, Culture and Development in Nigerian Enugu:ABIC Books, 2012.

Ward W.E.F. *Colonial Rule in West Africa,* Joseph C. Anene and Godfrey N. Brown eds. *Africa in the Nineteenth and Twentieth Centuries,* Ibadan: University Press, 1966.

Yinger, M.J. (1994), *Ethnicity: Source of Strength? Source of Conflict?*Albany/ N.Y. State University of New York Press.